Section 1: Online Marketplaces

1. Selling Used Items on eBay
2. Flipping Products on Amazon
3. Dropshipping
4. Selling Crafts on Etsy
5. Print on Demand (T-Shirts, Mugs, etc.)
6. Affiliate Marketing through Amazon Associates

Section 2: Content Creation and Writing

7. Blogging and Ad Revenue

1. Starting a YouTube Channel
2. Writing and Selling eBooks
3. Freelance Writing
4. Guest Blogging
5. Content Creation for Social Media

Section 3: Online Surveys and Reviews

13. Paid Online Surveys

1. Product Testing and Reviews

2. Sponsored Content on Social Media

3. Online Market Research

Section 4: Online Tutoring and Teaching

17. Online Tutoring

   1. Teach a Language
   2. Create Online Courses
   3. Educational YouTube Channel
   4. Virtual Dance or Fitness Classes

Section 5: Remote Work and Freelancing

22. Virtual Assistance

   1. Data Entry and Transcription
   2. Online Bookkeeping
   3. Graphic Design (Basic Skills)
   4. Social Media Management (Basic Skills)
   5. Virtual Event Planning

Section 6: Renting and Sharing

28. Rent Out Your Property on Airbnb

1. Car Sharing and Ridesharing
2. Rent Out Your Parking Space
3. Renting Photography Equipment

Section 7: Online Investments and Trading

32. Stock Market Investing (Basic)

1. Cryptocurrency Trading (Basic)
2. Peer-to-Peer Lending
3. Online Real Estate Investing

Section 8: Virtual Assistance and Admin Services

36. Virtual Receptionist Services

1. Online Data Entry
2. Email Management
3. Online Research
4. Social Media Moderation

Section 9: Art and Creative Ventures

41. Sell Art and Photography Online

  1. Design Custom Merchandise
  2. Voice Acting and Audio Narration
  3. Virtual Event DJ
  4. Online Karaoke Hosting

Section 10: Miscellaneous Online Opportunities

46. Microtasking and Gig Economy Platforms

  1. Cashback and Rewards Programs
  2. Online Contests and Competitions
  3. Pet Sitting and Dog Walking Apps
  4. Testing Websites and Apps for Usability

Introduction: Earning Money Online Without Professional Skills

In today's digital age, the internet has revolutionized the way we work and make a living. The exciting news is that you don't always need to possess professional skills or advanced degrees to start earning money online. This eBook is your gateway to discovering 50 easy ways to boost your income without the traditional barriers of formal qualifications or specialized expertise.

The Flexibility Advantage:

One of the remarkable aspects of earning money online is the unparalleled flexibility it offers. Unlike traditional 9-to-5 jobs, these online opportunities allow you to set your own hours, work from the comfort of your home, and even pursue multiple income streams simultaneously. Whether you're a stay-at-home parent, a student looking to cover expenses, or someone seeking additional income alongside their regular job, these methods can adapt to your lifestyle.

Accessibility for Everyone:

Another exciting feature of online income sources is their accessibility. With just a computer or smartphone and an internet connection, you can tap into a world of possibilities. These methods are open to people of all backgrounds, ages, and locations. You don't need a massive upfront investment, an expensive office space, or years of experience to get started. All you need is the willingness to explore, learn, and take action.

In this eBook, we'll explore various avenues that cater to different interests and goals. Whether you want to start a side hustle, create a passive income stream, or transition to a full-time online career, there's something here for you. From freelancing and e-commerce to passive income streams and specialized niches, the possibilities are vast.

So, if you've ever dreamed of enhancing your financial well-being without the constraints of traditional employment, you're in the right place. Let's embark on this journey together and discover how to make the most of the vast online landscape to earn money on your own terms.

1. Selling Used Items on eBay

eBay is one of the world's largest online marketplaces, and it provides an excellent platform for selling both new and used items. If you have items lying around that you no longer need, selling them on eBay can be a great way to declutter your space and earn some extra cash. Here's how to get started:

1.1. Gather Your Items:

Begin by identifying items in your home that you no longer use, such as clothing, electronics, collectibles, or vintage items. Make sure these items are in good condition.

1.2. Create an eBay Account:

If you don't already have one, sign up for an eBay account. It's a straightforward process that requires basic information.

1.3. Research Your Items:

Before listing your items, research similar products on eBay to gauge their market value. This will help you set competitive prices and attract potential buyers.

1.4. Create Detailed Listings:

When creating listings, provide clear and accurate descriptions of your items. Include high-quality photos from multiple angles to give buyers a good view of what they're purchasing. Mention any flaws or wear to build trust with buyers.

1.5. Set Your Pricing:

Decide whether you want to set a fixed price for your items or list them in auction-style listings, where potential buyers bid on them. Consider including a "Buy It Now" option for buyers who prefer immediate purchase.

1.6. Shipping and Payment:

Choose your preferred shipping options and clearly state shipping costs. eBay offers integrated shipping labels to simplify the process. Specify your accepted payment methods, including PayPal or credit cards.

1.7. Monitor Your Listings:

Keep an eye on your listings and promptly respond to questions from potential buyers. You can also adjust your prices or promotions if your items aren't selling as quickly as you'd like.

1.8. Complete the Sale:

Once your item sells, carefully package it and ship it to the buyer as soon as possible. eBay provides guidelines for safe and efficient shipping.

1.9. Handling Feedback:

Maintain a positive seller reputation by providing excellent customer service and accurately representing your items. Encourage satisfied buyers to leave positive feedback.

Selling used items on eBay is not only a way to make money but also a sustainable practice that helps reduce waste by giving new life to pre-owned goods. Whether you're looking to declutter, generate some extra income, or explore the world of online selling, eBay can be a valuable platform to consider. Just remember to be honest, responsive, and diligent in your selling efforts to build a trustworthy seller profile.

2. Flipping Products on Amazon

Flipping products on Amazon involves buying items at a lower price and then reselling them at a higher price on the Amazon platform. This method is commonly referred to as "retail arbitrage" or "online arbitrage." It can be a profitable venture with the potential to scale. Here's how you can get started:

2.1. Research and Product Selection:

Begin by researching products that are in demand on Amazon. Look for items with a consistent sales history and a gap between their selling price on Amazon and their cost elsewhere.

Consider sourcing products from various places, such as clearance sales, thrift stores, garage sales, liquidation sales, or even other online marketplaces.

2.2. Set Up an Amazon Seller Account:

If you don't have one already, sign up for an Amazon Seller account. You'll need to choose between an Individual or Professional selling plan based on your selling volume.

2.3. Analyze Profit Margins:

Calculate potential profits by factoring in the cost of the item, Amazon's fees, and shipping costs. Tools like Amazon's FBA Revenue Calculator can help with this.

2.4. List Your Products:

Create detailed listings for the products you intend to sell on Amazon. Include clear images, accurate descriptions, and competitive pricing.

You can choose to fulfill orders yourself (FBM - Fulfillment by Merchant) or let Amazon handle storage, packing, and shipping through Fulfillment by Amazon (FBA).

2.5. Monitor Your Inventory:

Keep track of your inventory levels to ensure you never run out of stock. Consistently replenish products that are selling well.

2.6. Competitive Pricing and Strategy:

Stay competitive by adjusting your prices as needed. Amazon's algorithm considers factors like price, seller reputation, and fulfillment method when ranking listings.

2.7. Customer Service:

Provide excellent customer service, including timely responses to inquiries and prompt shipping of orders. A positive seller reputation can boost sales.

2.8. Scaling Your Business:

As you gain experience and understanding of what sells well, consider scaling your operation by expanding into new product categories or sourcing from multiple suppliers.

It's important to note that while flipping products on Amazon can be profitable, it also comes with certain risks and challenges. Competition can be fierce, and Amazon's rules and fees may change over time. Therefore, staying informed and adapting to market dynamics are key to success in this endeavor.

2.9. Managing Returns and Customer Feedback:

Be prepared to handle returns and refunds professionally. Amazon values customer satisfaction, and handling returns effectively can help maintain a positive seller rating.

Encourage satisfied customers to leave reviews and feedback, as positive reviews can boost your visibility and sales.

2.10. Legal and Tax Considerations:

Familiarize yourself with the legal and tax aspects of running an Amazon selling business. This may include registering for sales tax in certain states or countries where you have a significant presence.

Keep detailed records of your income and expenses for tax reporting purposes.

2.11. Stay Informed:

The e-commerce landscape is continually evolving. Stay up-to-date with changes in Amazon's policies, fees, and marketplace dynamics. Join seller forums and follow industry news to remain informed.

2.12. Diversify Your Sourcing Channels:

While you may initially source products from physical retail stores, consider exploring other channels like online wholesalers, liquidation auctions, or manufacturer direct deals for a broader product selection.

Flipping products on Amazon can be a profitable endeavor, but it requires dedication, research, and careful execution. Remember that success in this business model often comes with time and experience. It's advisable to start small and gradually expand as you gain confidence and insights into what works best for you.

Keep in mind that while this method can yield excellent returns, it also involves an element of risk, as market conditions and product demand can change. Therefore, it's essential to be adaptable and willing to pivot your strategy when necessary.

Lastly, maintain a commitment to ethical business practices, outstanding customer service, and adherence to Amazon's policies. Building a strong seller reputation will contribute to your long-term success in the world of Amazon product flipping.

3. Dropshipping

Dropshipping is an e-commerce business model that allows you to sell products to customers without holding any inventory. Instead, when you make a sale, the product is shipped directly from your supplier to the customer. This model offers several advantages, including low startup costs and the ability to run your business from anywhere. Here's how to get started with dropshipping:

3.1. Choose a Niche and Products:

Select a niche or product category that interests you and has demand in the market. Conduct thorough research to identify products that are likely to sell well.

3.2. Find Reliable Suppliers:

Partner with reliable suppliers who offer dropshipping services. Popular options include AliExpress, SaleHoo, and Oberlo. Ensure your chosen suppliers have a good track record for quality and timely shipping.

3.3. Create an E-commerce Website:

You'll need an online store to showcase and sell your products. Options include setting up your own website using platforms like Shopify or using e-commerce marketplaces like eBay or Amazon.

3.4. Add Products to Your Store:

Import the products you want to sell from your chosen suppliers to your online store. Write compelling product descriptions and use high-quality images to attract potential customers.

3.5. Set Pricing and Policies:

Determine your pricing strategy, considering factors like product cost, shipping fees, and your desired profit margin. Establish clear policies for shipping times, returns, and customer support.

3.6. Market Your Store:

Use digital marketing strategies like search engine optimization (SEO), social media marketing, and pay-per-click advertising to drive traffic to your online store. Engage with your target audience through content marketing and email marketing.

3.7. Manage Orders:

When a customer places an order on your website, forward the order details to your supplier, who will then ship the product directly to the customer. Keep customers informed about order status and tracking information.

3.8. Customer Service:

Provide excellent customer service by promptly addressing inquiries, concerns, and returns. Building trust with your customers is crucial for long-term success.

3.9. Monitor and Optimize:

Continuously analyze your product performance, sales data, and customer feedback. Adjust your product selection and marketing strategies based on what works best.

3.10. Legal and Financial Considerations:

- Ensure you comply with all legal requirements and tax regulations for your business. Consult with a legal or financial advisor if needed.

Dropshipping can be a lucrative business model, but it's important to manage it carefully. While it offers low overhead costs and the freedom to run your business remotely, it also comes with challenges such as competition, supplier reliability, and the need for effective marketing.

3.11. Inventory Management:

Keep track of your product inventory, even though you don't physically handle the products. Ensure that you don't oversell items that are out of stock with your suppliers.

3.12. Handling Returns and Refunds:

Have a clear policy for handling returns and refunds, as customer satisfaction is essential. Communicate your return process to customers and work closely with your suppliers when processing returns.

3.13. Scaling Your Business:

As your dropshipping business grows, consider expanding your product range or exploring additional marketing channels. Scaling strategically can help increase your revenue and profitability.

3.14. Building Your Brand:

Over time, consider building your brand identity to differentiate yourself from competitors. This can include creating a unique logo, packaging, and cultivating a strong online presence.

3.15. Stay Informed and Adapt:

The e-commerce landscape is constantly changing. Stay informed about industry trends, competitor strategies, and changes in online marketplaces. Adapt your business strategies accordingly.

3.16. Diversify Suppliers:

To minimize risk and ensure product availability, consider working with multiple suppliers for the same or similar products. This can provide backup options if one supplier faces issues.

3.17. Customer Feedback and Reviews:

Encourage satisfied customers to leave reviews and feedback on your website or the platform you use. Positive reviews can boost credibility and attract more customers.

3.18. Evaluate Profit Margins:

Continually analyze your profit margins to ensure they meet your business goals. Adjust pricing or product selection if necessary to maintain profitability.

Dropshipping offers an accessible entry point into the world of e-commerce, making it a popular choice for aspiring entrepreneurs. While it can be a rewarding business model, it's important to approach it with realistic expectations and a commitment to providing excellent customer service.

Remember that building a successful dropshipping business may take time, effort, and a willingness to adapt to changing market conditions. Continuously educate yourself, stay updated on industry trends, and be prepared to adjust your strategies to achieve long-term success in the world of dropshipping.

4. Selling Crafts on Etsy

Etsy is a dedicated online marketplace for artisans, crafters, and creatives. If you have a talent for crafting unique handmade items or vintage goods, Etsy can be an ideal platform to showcase your creations and earn money. Here's how to get started:

4.1. Choose Your Craft Niche:

Identify your craft niche or the type of handmade items you want to sell on Etsy. This could include jewelry, clothing, home decor, art, candles, or any other craft you're passionate about.

4.2. Create a Unique Brand and Shop Name:

Establish a memorable brand name and shop identity that reflects your style and the essence of your craft. A catchy name can help you stand out in the Etsy marketplace.

4.3. Set Up Your Etsy Shop:

Sign up for an Etsy seller account if you don't have one. Creating a shop is a straightforward process that includes adding shop details, policies, and payment methods.

4.4. Craft High-Quality Products:

Craft your items with care and attention to detail. Quality and uniqueness are key factors that attract buyers on Etsy.

4.5. Create Stunning Product Listings:

Each product listing should feature high-quality photos that showcase your items from multiple angles. Write compelling and detailed descriptions that highlight the materials used, dimensions, and the story behind your craft.

4.6. Pricing Your Crafts:

Calculate your pricing by considering the cost of materials, labor, and your desired profit margin. Research similar items on Etsy to ensure your pricing is competitive.

4.7. Shipping and Packaging:

Determine your shipping methods and costs. Etsy offers tools to help you calculate shipping fees accurately. Invest in attractive and secure packaging to make a positive impression.

4.8. SEO Optimization:

Utilize Etsy's search engine optimization (SEO) tools to optimize your product listings. Use relevant keywords and tags to help potential buyers find your items in search results.

4.9. Promote Your Shop:

Share your shop and product listings on social media platforms, participate in Etsy teams and forums, and consider running paid Etsy ads to increase visibility.

4.10. Customer Engagement:

- Engage with customers by responding to inquiries promptly and providing excellent customer service. Encourage happy buyers to leave reviews.

4.11. Consistency and Updates:

- Regularly update your shop with new listings, refresh your product photos, and adjust your offerings based on trends and customer feedback.

4.12. Legal Considerations:

- Be aware of any legal obligations related to your crafts, such as copyright or safety regulations. Ensure that your items meet Etsy's policies.

Selling crafts on Etsy can be a fulfilling way to turn your creative passion into a source of income. While it may take time to build a customer base and establish your brand, the Etsy community appreciates unique, handmade items, and buyers often return for more. With dedication, attention to detail, and a commitment to quality, you can create a successful shop on Etsy and share your crafts with a global audience.

5. Print on Demand (T-Shirts, Mugs, etc.)

Print on demand (POD) is a popular e-commerce business model that allows you to create custom-designed products such as T-shirts, mugs, phone cases, and more without holding inventory. When a customer places an order, the product is printed and shipped directly from a POD provider. Here's how to get started:

5.1. Select Your Niche and Products:

Choose a niche or category of products you want to sell, such as clothing, accessories, home decor, or stationery. Consider products that align with your interests and target audience.

5.2. Research and Choose a POD Provider:

Research and select a reliable POD provider. Popular options include Printful,

Printify, and Teespring. Ensure the provider offers the products you want to sell and integrates with your chosen e-commerce platform.

5.3. Create Designs:

Design custom graphics, artwork, or slogans for your chosen products. You can create designs yourself or hire a freelance designer. Make sure your designs are unique and appealing to your target audience.

5.4. Set Up an E-commerce Store:

Create an online store to showcase your products and facilitate sales. E-commerce platforms like Shopify, WooCommerce, and Etsy offer integrations with POD providers.

5.5. Connect Your Store with the POD Provider:

Integrate your e-commerce platform with your chosen POD provider. This allows for seamless order processing and fulfillment.

5.6. Design Product Listings:

Create product listings for each item in your store. Include eye-catching product images that feature your designs and write engaging product descriptions.

5.7. Pricing and Profit Margins:

Determine your pricing strategy by considering the base cost of the product from the POD provider, your desired profit margin, and any additional costs like shipping and taxes.

5.8. Marketing and Promotion:

Promote your products through various marketing channels. Use social media, email marketing, paid advertising, and content marketing to reach your target audience.

5.9. Customer Service:

Provide excellent customer service by addressing inquiries promptly and professionally. Ensure clear communication about shipping times and returns.

5.10. Monitor Sales and Analytics:

- Keep track of your sales and monitor analytics to understand which products are popular and which marketing efforts are effective.

5.11. Expand Product Offerings:

- As your business grows, consider expanding your product line to cater to different tastes and trends. Continuously update your designs to stay fresh and appealing.

5.12. Legal Considerations:

- Ensure that your designs do not violate copyright or trademark laws. Respect intellectual property rights and create original content or secure proper licensing if needed.

5.13. Quality Assurance:

Maintain a high standard of quality for your products. Regularly review sample products from your POD provider to ensure that the printing, material, and product quality meet your standards.

5.14. Seasonal and Trend-Based Offerings:

Stay attuned to seasonal and trend-based opportunities. Create designs and products that align with holidays, special occasions, or emerging trends to attract a broader customer base.

5.15. Build an Engaged Audience:

Cultivate a community of followers and customers who resonate with your brand. Engage with your audience through social media, email newsletters, and content that adds value to their lives.

5.16. Collaborations and Partnerships:

Explore collaborations with influencers or other brands to expand your reach. Partnering with influencers can help promote your products to a larger and more targeted audience.

5.17. Manage Customer Expectations:

Be transparent about shipping times, especially during peak seasons. Manage customer expectations to reduce the likelihood of disappointment due to longer delivery times.

5.18. Reinvest in Your Business:

As your business grows, consider reinvesting profits into expanding your product range, improving marketing efforts, or enhancing your website's user experience.

5.19. Data Analytics and Optimization:

Utilize data analytics to identify trends, customer preferences, and areas for improvement. Optimize your product offerings and marketing strategies based on this data.

5.20. Diversify Sales Channels:

Consider expanding beyond your primary e-commerce store. Explore additional sales channels like Amazon Merch, eBay, or even physical pop-up shops if they align with your brand and audience.

Print on demand is a versatile and accessible way to turn your creative ideas into a thriving online business. It allows you to experiment with various designs and products without the overhead costs of traditional manufacturing. With dedication and a focus on quality, customer satisfaction, and adaptability, you can build a successful print-on-demand business that resonates with your target audience and generates a sustainable income.

6. Affiliate Marketing through Amazon Associates

Affiliate marketing is a performance-based marketing strategy where you earn commissions by promoting products or services from a merchant on your website, blog, or social media. Amazon Associates is one of the most popular affiliate programs globally, allowing you to earn a commission for driving sales to Amazon. Here's how to get started:

6.1. Sign Up for Amazon Associates:

Visit the Amazon Associates website and sign up for an account. You'll need an active website, blog, YouTube channel, or social media presence to apply.

6.2. Choose Your Niche:

Select a niche or category of products that align with your interests and expertise. It's essential to focus on a niche you are passionate about and knowledgeable in.

6.3. Create Content:

Start creating high-quality content that incorporates Amazon affiliate links naturally. This content can take the form of product reviews, how-to guides, listicles, or comparison articles.

6.4. Select Amazon Products:

Browse Amazon's vast product catalog to find products relevant to your niche. Use the Amazon Associates dashboard to generate affiliate links for these products.

6.5. Add Affiliate Links:

Integrate affiliate links into your content where appropriate. Make sure they blend seamlessly with your content, so they don't appear overly promotional.

6.6. Disclose Affiliate Relationships:

It's crucial to disclose your affiliate relationship with Amazon by including a clear and visible disclaimer on your website or content. This transparency builds trust with your audience.

6.7. Drive Traffic:

Promote your content through various channels, such as social media, email marketing, SEO optimization, or paid advertising, to attract relevant traffic to your website or platform.

6.8. Optimize for Conversions:

Experiment with different types of content, affiliate link placements, and call-to-actions to maximize conversion rates. Monitor which strategies work best for your audience.

6.9. Analyze Performance:

Use Amazon Associates' reporting tools to track the performance of your affiliate links. Analyze metrics such as clicks, conversions, and commissions earned.

6.10. Comply with Amazon's Policies:

- Familiarize yourself with Amazon's affiliate program policies to ensure compliance. Amazon may periodically update its terms and conditions, so stay informed.

6.11. Diversify Income Streams:

- Consider diversifying your income sources by partnering with other affiliate programs or monetization methods, such as display advertising or selling digital products.

6.12. Continuously Improve:

- Affiliate marketing is an evolving field. Stay updated on industry trends, SEO best practices, and content creation techniques to enhance your affiliate marketing efforts.

Affiliate marketing through Amazon Associates can be a lucrative way to monetize your website or online presence. While it may take time to build a substantial income, with consistent effort and a focus on creating valuable content for your audience, you can generate commissions by recommending products and services available on Amazon. Always prioritize delivering value to your audience and maintaining transparency about your affiliate relationships to build trust and credibility.

7. Blogging and Ad Revenue

Blogging is a versatile online venture that allows you to share your knowledge, expertise, or interests through written content. One of the primary ways bloggers monetize their websites is through ad revenue. Here's how to get started:

7.1. Choose Your Blog Niche:

Select a niche or topic that you're passionate about and knowledgeable in. Your niche should have an audience interested in the content you'll be producing.

7.2. Set Up Your Blog:

Register a domain name and choose a reliable web hosting provider. Popular blogging platforms include WordPress, Blogger, and Wix.

7.3. Create High-Quality Content:

Start writing and publishing high-quality, engaging content on your blog. Your content should provide value, solve problems, or entertain your target audience.

7.4. Build Your Audience:

Promote your blog through various channels, including social media, email newsletters, and search engine optimization (SEO). Engage with your readers through comments and feedback.

7.5. Apply for Ad Networks:

Once your blog starts receiving consistent traffic, you can apply to join ad networks. Google AdSense is a popular option for bloggers. Other ad networks like

Media.net and Ezoic are also worth considering.

7.6. Place Ads Strategically:

Integrate ad placements into your blog design strategically. Common ad placements include within content, in the sidebar, or at the header and footer of your website.

7.7. Optimize Ad Revenue:

Experiment with ad formats, sizes, and placements to find what works best for your audience. Monitor ad performance metrics such as click-through rates (CTR) and earnings per thousand impressions (eCPM).

7.8. Diversify Income Streams:

Besides ad revenue, consider other monetization methods such as affiliate marketing, sponsored content, selling digital products, or offering online courses.

7.9. Balance User Experience:

Be mindful of user experience (UX) by avoiding excessive ads that disrupt your readers' experience. A clutter-free, well-designed blog is more likely to retain readers.

7.10. Analyze and Iterate:

- Use website analytics tools to track your blog's performance. Analyze which content resonates most with your audience and refine your content strategy accordingly.

7.11. Stay Consistent:

- Consistency is key in blogging. Maintain a regular posting schedule to keep your audience engaged and returning for more.

7.12. Legal and Ethical Considerations:

- Adhere to legal and ethical guidelines for blogging, including disclosure of affiliate relationships and adherence to copyright and privacy laws.

7.13. Patience and Persistence:

- Building a profitable blog and earning substantial ad revenue takes time. Stay patient, keep learning, and adapt to changes in the blogging landscape.

Blogging and ad revenue can be a rewarding way to turn your passion for writing and expertise into income. It offers the flexibility to write about topics you love while monetizing your blog's traffic through ad networks and other revenue streams. By providing value to your audience and continually improving your content and website, you can build a successful blog and generate a steady stream of ad revenue over time.

8. Starting a YouTube Channel

YouTube is one of the world's largest video-sharing platforms, offering immense potential for content creators to reach a global audience and generate income. Here's how to get started with your own YouTube channel:

8.1. Choose Your Niche and Content:

Identify a niche or topic that you're passionate about and knowledgeable in. This niche should have an audience interested in the content you plan to create.

8.2. Create a Google Account:

If you don't already have one, create a Google account. This account will be used to access YouTube and its various features.

8.3. Set Up Your YouTube Channel:

Sign in to YouTube and click on the user icon in the top right corner. Then, select "Your Channel" to create and customize your channel. Add a profile picture, banner, and channel description.

8.4. Plan and Create Content:

Develop a content strategy and plan your video topics. Start creating high-quality videos that provide value, entertain, or educate your target audience.

8.5. Invest in Equipment and Software:

Invest in decent video and audio equipment to ensure your videos are of good quality. You'll need a camera (can be a smartphone with a good camera), microphone, and video editing software.

8.6. Optimize Video Titles and Descriptions:

Optimize your video titles, descriptions, and tags for search engine optimization (SEO). Use relevant keywords to make your videos discoverable.

8.7. Upload and Publish Regularly:

Consistency is key on YouTube. Publish videos on a regular schedule to keep your audience engaged and returning for more.

8.8. Build Your Audience:

Promote your YouTube channel on social media, engage with your viewers through comments and community posts, and encourage subscriptions and notifications.

8.9. Monetize Your Channel:

To earn money through YouTube, you can apply for the YouTube Partner Program (YPP) when you meet its eligibility requirements, including having 1,000 subscribers and 4,000 watch hours in the past 12 months.

8.10. Explore Monetization Options:

- Once accepted into the YPP, you can earn revenue through various monetization methods, including ads, channel memberships, merchandise shelf, Super Chat, and YouTube Premium revenue.

8.11. Protect Your Content:

- Familiarize yourself with copyright and fair use laws. Create original content or ensure you have the necessary permissions to use copyrighted materials.

8.12. Engage with Your Community:

- Respond to comments and engage with your viewers to build a loyal and supportive community around your channel.

8.13. Analyze and Improve:

- Use YouTube analytics to track the performance of your videos and audience engagement. Use this data to refine your content strategy and improve your channel over time.

8.14. Stay Informed:

- YouTube is continuously evolving, with changes in policies and algorithms. Stay informed about industry trends and updates from YouTube to adapt your strategies.

Starting a YouTube channel is a creative and potentially lucrative endeavor. It allows you to share your knowledge, talents, and passions with a vast online audience. By consistently delivering valuable and engaging content, optimizing your videos for search, and building a loyal community, you can grow your YouTube channel and generate income through various monetization methods. Remember that success on YouTube often requires patience, persistence, and adaptability to changing trends and audience preferences.

9. Writing and Selling eBooks

Writing and selling eBooks is a popular way to share your knowledge, creativity, or expertise with a global audience while generating income. Whether you're a seasoned author or a first-time writer, here are the steps to get started:

9.1. Choose Your eBook Niche:

Identify a niche or topic that you're passionate about and knowledgeable in. Your eBook should provide value or entertainment to your target audience.

9.2. Research and Outline:

Research your chosen topic thoroughly. Create an outline or a structure for your eBook to organize your content effectively.

9.3. Write Your eBook:

Start writing your eBook based on your outline. Focus on producing high-quality, well-structured content that engages your readers.

9.4. Edit and Proofread:

Editing is crucial. Edit your eBook for grammar, spelling, and clarity. Consider hiring a professional editor or proofreader for a polished final product.

9.5. Design the eBook:

Invest in professional eBook formatting and cover design. A visually appealing eBook is more likely to attract readers.

9.6. Choose a Distribution Platform:

Decide where you want to sell your eBook. Popular eBook distribution platforms include Amazon Kindle Direct Publishing (KDP), Apple Books, Google Play Books, and Smashwords.

9.7. Set a Price:

Determine the price for your eBook. Consider factors like your niche, competition, and the perceived value of your content.

9.8. Publish Your eBook:

Format your eBook according to the requirements of your chosen distribution platform and publish it. Ensure you follow all publishing guidelines.

9.9. Market Your eBook:

Promote your eBook through various channels, including social media, your website or blog, email marketing, and online communities related to your niche.

9.10. Leverage Amazon Kindle Select (Optional):

- If you publish on Amazon KDP, you can enroll your eBook in Kindle Select, which offers promotional opportunities and access to Kindle Unlimited subscribers.

9.11. Encourage Reviews:

- Encourage readers to leave reviews for your eBook, as positive reviews can boost credibility and visibility.

9.12. Analyze Sales and Adjust:

- Use sales data and analytics from your chosen distribution platform to track your eBook's performance. Adjust your marketing and pricing strategies as needed.

9.13. Consider Other Formats:

- If your eBook is successful, consider offering it in other formats like audiobooks or print-on-demand paperbacks for additional revenue streams.

9.14. Protect Your Work:

- Consider copyright protection and look into legal considerations for your eBook, including licensing and distribution rights.

9.15. Build an Author Brand:

- If you plan to write more eBooks in the future, consider building an author brand to gain recognition and attract a loyal readership.

Writing and selling eBooks is an accessible way to share your knowledge or creativity and potentially earn a steady income. Success in this endeavor often comes with persistence, a commitment to quality, and effective marketing strategies. Keep in mind that the eBook market is competitive, so focus on delivering unique and valuable content that resonates with your target audience. With time and effort, you can build a portfolio of eBooks that generate ongoing revenue.

10. Freelance Writing

Freelance writing is a flexible and accessible way to earn money online by offering your writing skills and expertise to clients who need content for various purposes. Whether you're a seasoned writer or just starting, here's how to begin your freelance writing career:

10.1. Build a Writing Portfolio:

Before seeking clients, create a portfolio of your best writing samples. These can be articles, blog posts, essays, or any type of content that showcases your writing skills.

10.2. Define Your Niche and Expertise:

Identify your writing niche or areas of expertise. Specializing in a particular field, such as technology, health, finance, or travel, can make you more appealing to clients in that niche.

10.3. Set Your Rates:

Determine your freelance writing rates based on factors like your experience, expertise, and the type of content you'll be producing. Research industry standards to ensure your rates are competitive.

10.4. Create a Professional Online Presence:

Build a professional website or blog that showcases your writing services, portfolio, and contact information. An online presence adds credibility and helps potential clients find you.

10.5. Join Freelance Job Platforms:

Sign up for freelance job platforms like Upwork, Freelancer, Guru, or Fiverr. These platforms connect freelance writers with clients seeking content.

10.6. Create a Compelling Profile:

Craft a detailed and engaging profile on freelance job platforms. Highlight your skills, experience, and expertise. Use a professional profile picture.

10.7. Search for Writing Jobs:

Browse job listings on freelance platforms to find writing opportunities that match your skills and interests. Apply to relevant jobs by submitting tailored proposals.

10.8. Network and Market Yourself:

Promote your freelance writing services through social media, professional networks like LinkedIn, and by attending industry events or writing conferences.

10.9. Deliver Quality Work:

Once you secure a freelance writing project, communicate effectively with the client to understand their requirements. Deliver high-quality, well-researched, and error-free content on time.

10.10. Handle Revisions and Feedback:

- Be open to client feedback and willing to make revisions to your work as needed. Building a positive working relationship can lead to repeat business.

10.11. Manage Your Finances:

- Keep track of your earnings and expenses for tax purposes. Consider setting up a dedicated business bank account and consult with a tax advisor if necessary.

10.12. Expand Your Skill Set:

- Continuously improve your writing skills and consider diversifying your services. You might explore content marketing, SEO writing, technical writing, or copywriting, depending on your interests.

10.13. Build Long-Term Relationships:

- Nurture long-term relationships with clients who appreciate your work. Repeat clients can provide a stable source of income and referrals.

10.14. Protect Your Work:

- Consider using contracts to outline project terms, deadlines, and payment details. This can help protect both you and your clients.

Freelance writing offers the opportunity to turn your writing passion into a profitable online career. Success in freelance writing often comes with consistent effort, professionalism, and a dedication to delivering high-quality content. As you build your portfolio and reputation, you can attract more clients and potentially earn a steady income as a freelance writer.

11. Guest Blogging

Guest blogging is a valuable strategy for writers and bloggers to expand their reach, establish authority in their niche, and earn recognition within the online community. It involves writing articles or blog posts for other websites or blogs. Here's how to get started with guest blogging:

11.1. Identify Your Target Audience:

Determine the audience you want to reach and the topics that interest them. Guest blog posts should align with the host blog's audience.

11.2. Research Guest Blogging Opportunities:

Look for websites or blogs in your niche that accept guest contributions. You can find these opportunities through Google searches, social media, or platforms like "My Blog Guest" and "GuestPost."

11.3. Read and Familiarize Yourself:

Before pitching guest posts, thoroughly read the host blog's content to understand its tone, style, and audience preferences. Tailor your guest post accordingly.

11.4. Craft a Pitch:

Contact the host blog or website with a well-crafted pitch. Your pitch should include your proposed topic, a brief summary of your credentials, and why your post would benefit their audience.

11.5. Write High-Quality Content:

Once your pitch is accepted, create a well-researched and engaging guest post. Focus on providing value and unique insights to the host blog's readers.

11.6. Follow Submission Guidelines:

Pay close attention to the host blog's submission guidelines, including word count, formatting, and any specific requirements. Adhering to these guidelines is essential for a smooth publishing process.

11.7. Include a Bio and Links:

In your guest post, include a brief author bio that introduces yourself and your expertise. You can typically include one or more links to your own website or social media profiles.

11.8. Engage with Readers:

Once your guest post is published, engage with readers in the comments section. Answer questions, provide additional insights, and build connections with the host blog's audience.

11.9. Promote Your Guest Post:

- Share your guest post on your own social media channels and website to maximize its exposure. This also shows appreciation to the host blog for featuring your content.

11.10. Build Relationships:

- Cultivate relationships with the editors or owners of the blogs where you guest post. Building connections can lead to more guest blogging opportunities and collaborations in the future.

11.11. Measure Impact:

- Monitor the impact of your guest posts by tracking website traffic, engagement, and any growth in your own audience or subscriber base.

11.12. Be Consistent:

- Keep guest blogging as a consistent part of your content strategy. Regular contributions can enhance your online presence and authority in your niche.

Guest blogging is a powerful tool for building your online presence, connecting with a broader audience, and establishing yourself as an expert in your field. Over time, it can lead to increased website traffic, recognition, and potential collaborations with other bloggers and websites. Remember that guest blogging is a two-way street, and providing value to the host blog's audience is key to its success.

12 Content Creation for Social Media

12.1. Define Your Social Media Strategy: Determine your social media goals. Are you looking to increase brand awareness, drive website traffic, generate leads, or engage with your audience?

Identify your target audience. Understand their interests, preferences, and demographics to tailor your content effectively.

Choose the social media platforms that align with your goals and target audience. Popular options include Facebook, Instagram, Twitter, LinkedIn, Pinterest, and TikTok.

12.2. Content Planning and Calendar:

Develop a content calendar to plan your posts in advance. This helps maintain consistency and ensures you cover a variety of topics.

Create a content mix that includes various types of posts, such as informational, promotional, educational, and entertaining content.

Schedule posts at optimal times to reach your target audience. You can use social media management tools like Buffer or Hootsuite to schedule posts.

12.3. Content Creation Tips:

Create visually appealing content by using high-quality images and graphics.

Use concise and engaging captions that encourage interaction.

Experiment with different content formats, such as videos, infographics, carousels, and live streams.

Maintain a consistent brand voice and style across all your social media channels.

Be authentic and relatable in your content to connect with your audience on a personal level.

12.4. Content Ideas for Social Media:

Share behind-the-scenes glimpses of your business or personal life to humanize your brand.

Create how-to tutorials and educational content related to your niche.

Showcase user-generated content or customer testimonials.

Share industry news, trends, and relevant articles.

Host contests, giveaways, and interactive polls or quizzes.

Use storytelling to convey your brand's mission, values, and journey.

12.5. Engage and Respond:

Regularly monitor your social media accounts for comments, messages, and mentions.

Engage with your audience by responding promptly and authentically.

Encourage discussions and conversations in the comments section of your posts.

Address both positive and negative feedback professionally and constructively.

12.6. Analyze and Adjust:

Use analytics tools provided by social media platforms or third-party tools to track the performance of your posts.

Measure key metrics like engagement rates, reach, click-through rates, and follower growth.

Adjust your content strategy based on what performs well and what doesn't.

12.7. Advertising on Social Media:

Consider using paid advertising options on social media platforms to reach a broader audience and target specific demographics.

Set clear objectives and budgets for your social media advertising campaigns.

A/B test different ad creatives and targeting options to optimize your campaigns.

12.8. Stay Informed:

Stay updated on social media trends, algorithm changes, and new features. Social media platforms are constantly evolving, so adapt your strategy accordingly.

Creating content for social media is an ongoing process that requires creativity, consistency, and a deep understanding of your audience. By crafting engaging content, maintaining an active presence, and continuously analyzing and improving your strategy, you can effectively leverage social media to achieve your goals, whether they're related to brand awareness, engagement, or conversions.

13. Paid Online Surveys

Paid online surveys offer a simple way to earn money or rewards by providing your opinions and feedback on various topics and products. Here's how to get started with paid online surveys:

13.1. Sign Up with Legitimate Survey Sites:

Begin by researching and signing up for reputable paid survey websites. Some well-known options include Swagbucks, Survey Junkie, Vindale Research, and Pinecone Research.

13.2. Create a Dedicated Email Address:

Consider creating a separate email address for survey invitations to keep your personal inbox organized.

13.3. Complete Your Profile:

After signing up, fill out your profile thoroughly. Survey sites use this information to match you with relevant survey opportunities.

13.4. Verify Legitimacy:

Be cautious of survey sites that ask for upfront fees or promise high earnings. Legitimate survey sites are free to join, and they provide clear information about compensation.

13.5. Participate Actively:

Log in to your survey accounts regularly to check for available surveys. Some surveys have limited slots and fill up quickly.

13.6. Be Honest and Accurate:

Answer survey questions honestly and accurately. Inconsistent or dishonest responses may result in account suspension.

13.7. Be Patient:

Earnings from paid surveys can vary. It may take some time to accumulate a substantial amount.

13.8. Explore Other Earning Opportunities:

Some survey sites offer additional earning opportunities, such as watching videos, participating in focus groups, or testing products.

13.9. Cash Out or Redeem Rewards:

Once you reach the minimum payout threshold, you can cash out your earnings via PayPal or choose from various gift cards or merchandise options, depending on the survey site.

13.10. Be Wary of Scams:

Be cautious of survey sites that make unrealistic promises or request sensitive personal information.

13.11. Manage Your Time:

While paid surveys can be a convenient way to earn extra income, it's essential to manage your time effectively to balance survey-taking with other commitments.

13.12. Stay Informed:

Keep an eye on your survey accounts for updates and new opportunities.

Paid online surveys can be a straightforward way to earn a bit of extra income or receive rewards for sharing your opinions. While the earnings may not replace a full-time income, they can be a convenient way to make some additional money in your spare time. Remember to focus on reputable survey sites, be honest in your responses, and manage your expectations regarding earnings.

14. Product Testing and Reviews

Product testing and reviewing can be an enjoyable way to receive free products and potentially earn income by sharing your opinions and experiences with a wider audience. Here's how to get started:

14.1. Sign Up with Product Testing Websites:

Research and sign up for legitimate product testing websites and platforms. Some popular options include Influenster, Smiley360, BzzAgent, and Product Testing USA.

14.2. Create a Detailed Profile:

Complete your profile on these platforms, providing accurate and detailed information about your demographics, interests, and preferences. This information helps match you with suitable product testing opportunities.

14.3. Apply for Product Testing Campaigns:

Browse available product testing campaigns on these platforms and apply for those that interest you. Some campaigns may require you to answer surveys or questionnaires to determine your eligibility.

14.4. Receive and Test Products:

If you're selected for a campaign, you'll receive the product to test at home. Follow the instructions provided and use the product as directed.

14.5. Provide Feedback and Reviews:

After testing the product, share your honest feedback and experiences. This may involve writing a review, taking photos, or creating video content, depending on the campaign requirements.

14.6. Engage on Social Media:

Many product testing campaigns require participants to share their reviews and experiences on social media platforms. Use relevant hashtags and tags to reach a wider audience.

14.7. Build Your Reviewer Reputation:

Consistently participate in product testing campaigns and provide high-quality reviews. Building a positive reputation as a reviewer can lead to more opportunities.

14.8. Explore Paid Review Opportunities:

Some platforms offer paid review opportunities in addition to free products.

These paid opportunities may involve writing sponsored reviews or creating sponsored content.

14.9. Be Honest and Transparent:

Always provide honest and transparent reviews. Your credibility as a reviewer is essential, and dishonest reviews can harm your reputation.

14.10. Check for Tax Implications:

Depending on your location and the value of the products you receive, there may be tax implications. It's advisable to consult with a tax professional to ensure compliance.

14.11. Be Patient:

Product testing campaigns can vary in frequency and availability. Be patient and persistent in applying for campaigns that align with your interests.

14.12. Leverage Your Expertise:

If you have expertise in a specific niche (e.g., technology, beauty, fitness), consider focusing your product testing and reviewing efforts within that niche.

Product testing and reviewing can be a fun and rewarding way to try new products and share your opinions with others. While it may not provide a full-time income, it can lead to receiving a variety of free products and, in some cases, earning money through paid review opportunities. Building a strong online presence as a reviewer can also open doors to collaborations with brands and further opportunities in the future.

15. Sponsored Content on Social Media

Sponsored content on social media is a way to collaborate with brands and businesses to promote their products or services to your audience. It can be a lucrative income stream for influencers, bloggers, and content creators. Here's how to get started with sponsored content on social media:

15.1. Build Your Social Media Presence:

Focus on growing your social media following and engagement. Brands are more likely to collaborate with influencers who have an engaged and relevant audience.

15.2. Define Your Niche:

Identify your niche or area of expertise. This helps you attract brands that align with your content and audience.

15.3. Create High-Quality Content:

Consistently produce high-quality and visually appealing content that showcases your style and personality. Showcase your creativity and authenticity.

15.4. Engage with Your Audience:

Build a strong relationship with your followers by responding to comments, hosting Q&A sessions, and actively engaging with your audience.

15.5. Build a Media Kit:

Create a media kit that includes information about your social media channels, audience demographics, engagement rates, and examples of your best work.

15.6. Join Influencer Marketing Platforms:

Sign up for influencer marketing platforms like AspireIQ, Influencity, or BrandSnob. These platforms connect influencers with brands looking for collaborations.

15.7. Outreach to Brands:

Reach out to brands or businesses that align with your niche and values. Craft personalized pitches that highlight how your audience can benefit them.

15.8. Understand FTC Guidelines:

Familiarize yourself with the Federal Trade Commission (FTC) guidelines regarding sponsored content. Always disclose your paid partnerships to maintain transparency with your audience.

15.9. Negotiate Terms and Compensation:

Negotiate the terms of the collaboration, including deliverables, compensation, timeline, and exclusivity clauses. Ensure both parties agree on the terms before proceeding.

15.10. Create Engaging Sponsored Content:

Develop creative and engaging sponsored content that seamlessly integrates the brand's product or message into your usual content style.

15.11. Promote Ethical Brand Partnerships:

Choose brand partnerships that align with your values and resonate with your audience. Promoting products or services you genuinely believe in fosters authenticity.

15.12. Monitor and Measure Performance:

Track the performance of your sponsored content using analytics provided by the social media platform or third-party tools. Share the results with your brand partners.

15.13. Build Long-Term Relationships:

Foster long-term relationships with brands that appreciate your work. Repeat collaborations with the same brands can provide stability and consistent income.

15.14. Diversify Your Income:

While sponsored content can be a significant income source, consider diversifying your income through other monetization methods like affiliate marketing, merchandise sales, or digital products.

Sponsored content on social media can be a rewarding way to monetize your online presence and collaborate with brands you admire. Success in this space often comes from building a strong personal brand, maintaining authenticity, and nurturing relationships with both your audience and brand partners.

16. Online Market Research

Online market research is a valuable way to earn money by participating in surveys, focus groups, and studies that help companies gather data and insights about consumer preferences and behavior. Here's how to get started with online market research:

16.1. Sign Up with Legitimate Market Research Companies:

Start by signing up with reputable market research companies and platforms. Some well-known options include SurveyMonkey, Ipsos i-Say, and Toluna.

16.2. Create a Dedicated Email Address:

Consider creating a separate email address for market research invitations to keep your primary inbox organized.

16.3. Complete Your Profile:

After signing up, fill out your profile honestly and thoroughly. Your profile information helps match you with relevant research opportunities.

16.4. Participate Actively:

Regularly check your email or the market research platform for available surveys, focus groups, or studies. Act quickly, as some opportunities have limited slots.

16.5. Be Honest and Accurate:

Provide truthful and accurate responses when participating in surveys or studies. Consistency and honesty are important for maintaining your eligibility.

16.6. Be Patient:

Earnings from online market research can vary. It may take time to accumulate a significant amount of money or rewards.

16.7. Explore Other Opportunities:

Some market research platforms offer additional earning opportunities, such as participating in online focus groups or testing new products.

16.8. Cash Out or Redeem Rewards:

Once you reach the minimum payout threshold or accumulate enough points, you can cash out your earnings or redeem them for gift cards or merchandise, depending on the platform.

16.9. Protect Your Personal Information:

Be cautious when sharing personal information. Legitimate market research companies should not ask for sensitive information like your social security number or financial details.

16.10. Be Wary of Scams:

Beware of market research opportunities that promise unusually high earnings or ask for upfront fees. Legitimate market research should not cost you money.

16.11. Check for Tax Implications:

Depending on your location and the value of the rewards or earnings, there may be tax implications. Consult with a tax professional if necessary.

16.12. Stay Informed:

Keep an eye on your market research accounts for updates and new opportunities.

Online market research can be a convenient way to earn extra income or receive rewards for sharing your opinions and feedback. While it may not replace a full-time income, it can provide additional financial support or help you earn gift cards and other valuable rewards. Remember to focus on legitimate market research companies, be honest in your responses, and manage your expectations regarding earnings.

17. Online Tutoring

Online tutoring is a rewarding way to share your knowledge and expertise while earning money from the comfort of your home. Whether you're an expert in a specific subject or skill, or you have teaching experience, here's how to get started with online tutoring:

17.1. Identify Your Niche and Expertise:

Determine the subjects or skills you are knowledgeable in and passionate about. This will help you target a specific audience and market your tutoring services effectively.

17.2. Choose Your Online Tutoring Platform:

Decide whether you want to work independently or join an online tutoring platform. Popular platforms include Wyzant, Chegg Tutors, VIPKid (for teaching English), and Tutor.com.

17.3. Set Your Rates:

Determine your tutoring rates based on factors like your qualifications, experience, and the demand for your expertise. Research rates in your niche to stay competitive.

17.4. Create a Professional Profile:

If you're using an online tutoring platform, create a detailed and professional profile. Highlight your qualifications, educational background, teaching style, and any certifications.

17.5. Prepare Teaching Materials:

Develop teaching materials and resources that align with your tutoring sessions. This can include lesson plans, worksheets, and additional study materials.

17.6. Advertise Your Services:

Promote your online tutoring services through your own website, social media, and professional networks. Let friends, family, and acquaintances know about your tutoring business.

17.7. Schedule Your Sessions:

Set up a schedule that works for you and your students. Consider different time zones if you plan to tutor students from around the world.

17.8. Conduct Effective Tutoring Sessions:

During your sessions, be patient, attentive, and adaptable to your students' learning needs. Use various teaching methods to cater to different learning styles.

17.9. Offer Free Consultations:

Consider offering a free consultation session to potential students. This can help both you and the student assess compatibility and learning goals.

17.10. Gather Feedback:

Encourage students to provide feedback on your tutoring sessions. Use this feedback to improve your teaching methods and materials.

17.11. Stay Updated:

Stay informed about developments in your subject area and teaching techniques. Continuing education and professional development can enhance your tutoring skills.

17.12. Handle Payments and Taxes:

Determine your preferred method of receiving payments and keep track of your earnings for tax purposes. Consider consulting with a tax professional for guidance.

17.13. Legal Considerations:

Depending on your location and the age of your students, there may be legal requirements or background checks needed for online tutoring. Research local regulations and comply as necessary.

Online tutoring offers the flexibility to set your own schedule, work with students worldwide, and make a positive impact on their learning journey. Building a strong reputation as an online tutor takes time, but with dedication, professionalism, and effective teaching methods, you can establish a successful online tutoring business and help students achieve their academic or skill development goals.

18. Teach a Language Online

Teaching a language online is a rewarding way to share your language skills and culture with learners around the world while earning income. Whether you're fluent in English, Spanish, French, or any other language, here's how to get started with teaching a language online:

18.1. Choose Your Target Language:

Identify the language you are proficient in and passionate about teaching. This will determine your target audience and the market for your lessons.

18.2. Determine Your Teaching Method:

Decide on your teaching approach. Will you offer conversational practice, formal lessons, exam preparation, or cultural immersion? Tailor your method to your students' needs.

18.3. Set Up Your Online Teaching Space:

Create a dedicated and well-lit teaching space in your home. Ensure you have a reliable internet connection, a computer with a webcam, and any necessary teaching materials.

18.4. Choose Your Online Teaching Platform:

Decide whether you want to teach independently or join an online language teaching platform. Platforms like iTalki, Verbling, Preply, and VIPKid offer opportunities for language tutors.

18.5. Set Your Rates:

Determine your tutoring rates based on your qualifications, experience, and market demand. Research the rates for language tutors in your niche to set competitive prices.

18.6. Create a Professional Profile:

If you're using a language teaching platform, create a detailed profile that highlights your qualifications, teaching style, and any relevant certifications.

18.7. Promote Your Services:

Market your language teaching services through social media, your website or blog, and online language learning communities. Networking and word-of-mouth referrals can also be valuable.

18.8. Prepare Lesson Plans:

Develop lesson plans and teaching materials that cater to your students' proficiency levels and goals. Plan interactive and engaging lessons to keep students motivated.

18.9. Offer Free Trial Lessons:

Consider offering free trial lessons to attract potential students. This allows them to experience your teaching style before committing.

18.10. Schedule Your Lessons:

Set up a flexible schedule that accommodates your students' time zones and availability. Be punctual and reliable in scheduling and conducting lessons.

18.11. Personalize Learning:

Tailor your lessons to meet each student's specific needs and goals. Provide feedback and support to help them progress.

18.12. Encourage Practice and Immersion:

Encourage students to practice outside of lessons by immersing themselves in the language. Recommend language-learning apps, books, movies, or cultural resources.

18.13. Gather Feedback:

Request feedback from your students to continually improve your teaching methods and materials.

18.14. Handle Payments and Taxes:

Determine your preferred method for receiving payments and keep records of your earnings for tax purposes. Comply with tax regulations in your area.

18.15. Legal Considerations:

Depending on your location and the age of your students, there may be legal requirements or background checks needed for online language teaching. Research and comply with local regulations.

Teaching a language online offers the opportunity to connect with language learners worldwide and help them achieve their language goals. Building a positive reputation as a language tutor requires dedication, adaptability, and effective teaching methods. With the right approach, you can establish a successful online language teaching business and make a meaningful impact on your students' language proficiency and cultural understanding.

19. Create Online Courses

Creating and selling online courses is an excellent way to share your expertise, knowledge, or skills with a global audience while generating income. Whether you're an expert in a specific field or have valuable insights to offer, here's how to get started with creating and selling online courses:

19.1. Choose Your Course Topic:

Identify a subject or topic that you are knowledgeable about and passionate about teaching. Ensure there is a demand for your chosen topic.

19.2. Conduct Market Research:

Research the competition and demand for similar courses. Look for gaps or unique angles that you can offer in your course.

19.3. Define Your Learning Objectives:

Clearly outline the learning objectives and outcomes that students can expect from your course. This will help you structure your content effectively.

19.4. Plan Your Course Content:

Create a comprehensive course outline that breaks down the content into modules or sections. Include lectures, assignments, quizzes, and any additional resources.

19.5. Choose a Platform:

Decide whether you want to host your course on a dedicated e-learning platform (e.g., Udemy, Teachable, Thinkific) or your own website using a learning management system (LMS).

19.6. Create Course Content:

Develop engaging and informative course materials, including video lectures, written content, quizzes, assignments, and downloadable resources.

19.7. Record Video Lectures:

If your course includes video content, invest in quality recording equipment, a good microphone, and video editing software to ensure professional-looking and sounding videos.

19.8. Design Course Materials:

Make your course visually appealing by using graphics, images, and slides where appropriate. Ensure the course layout is user-friendly and easy to navigate.

19.9. Set a Price:

Determine the pricing strategy for your course. Consider factors like the course's depth, competition, and your target audience's budget.

19.10. Create Marketing Materials:

Develop a marketing plan to promote your course. Create persuasive sales pages, video trailers, and promotional materials to attract potential students.

19.11. Build an Email List:

Build and nurture an email list of potential students interested in your course. Use email marketing to communicate course updates and promotions.

19.12. Launch Your Course:

Set a launch date and create buzz around your course. Consider offering an early-bird discount or bonuses for early enrollees.

19.13. Provide Support and Engagement:

Offer support to your students through discussion forums, email, or live Q&A sessions. Engage with your students to create a sense of community.

19.14. Gather Feedback:

Encourage students to provide feedback to help improve the course. Consider making updates or additions based on their suggestions.

19.15. Market Your Course Continuously:

Continue marketing your course through various channels, such as social media, content marketing, and partnerships with other influencers or websites.

19.16. Monitor Performance:

Track the performance of your course using analytics provided by your chosen platform or third-party tools. Analyze student engagement, completion rates, and feedback.

19.17. Offer Additional Resources:

Consider offering supplementary resources, such as ebooks, webinars, or one-on-one coaching, to enhance the learning experience and generate additional income.

Creating and selling online courses requires dedication, effective teaching methods, and ongoing marketing efforts. With the right approach, you can build a successful online course business that not only generates income but also provides valuable knowledge and skills to your students.

20. Creating an Educational YouTube Channel

Starting an educational YouTube channel is a fantastic way to share your knowledge, expertise, and passion with a wide audience while potentially earning income through ads, sponsorships, or merchandise. Here's how to get started:

20.1. Choose Your Educational Niche:

Select a specific educational niche or subject that you are passionate about and knowledgeable in. This will help you stand out in a crowded space.

20.2. Research Your Target Audience:

Understand your target audience's needs, interests, and preferences. Tailor your content to provide value to your viewers.

20.3. Plan Your Content:

Create a content plan or editorial calendar outlining the topics, titles, and formats of your videos. Plan a mix of beginner-friendly and advanced content.

20.4. Gather Equipment and Software:

Invest in essential equipment such as a good-quality camera, microphone, lighting, and video editing software to ensure professional-looking and sounding videos.

20.5. Create Engaging Content:

Craft informative, engaging, and visually appealing videos. Use storytelling techniques, visual aids, and clear explanations to captivate your audience.

20.6. Optimize Video SEO:

Implement effective video search engine optimization (SEO) techniques, including using relevant keywords in video titles, descriptions, and tags.

20.7. Upload Regularly:

Consistency is key on YouTube. Establish a publishing schedule and stick to it to keep your audience engaged and returning for more.

20.8. Interact with Your Audience:

Engage with your viewers by responding to comments, conducting Q&A sessions, and asking for feedback or video suggestions.

20.9. Create Eye-Catching Thumbnails:

Design compelling thumbnails that accurately represent your video content and entice viewers to click on your videos.

20.10. Monetize Your Channel:

Once you meet YouTube's eligibility requirements (such as 1,000 subscribers and 4,000 watch hours in the past year), consider enabling monetization through ads.

20.11. Explore Sponsorships and Merchandise:

As your channel grows, explore sponsorships, partnerships, and merchandise opportunities with brands and products relevant to your niche.

20.12. Build a Community:

Foster a sense of community among your viewers by creating a brand identity, a recognizable logo or banner, and even merchandise featuring your channel's branding.

20.13. Analyze Performance:

Use YouTube Analytics to monitor your video performance, including watch time, audience retention, and demographics. Adjust your content strategy based on these insights.

20.14. Collaborate with Others:

Collaborate with other YouTubers or experts in your field to reach a broader audience and introduce fresh perspectives.

20.15. Stay Informed and Adapt:

Stay updated on YouTube trends, algorithm changes, and best practices to adapt your content strategy accordingly.

Remember that building a successful educational YouTube channel takes time and effort. Focus on delivering high-quality, informative content that genuinely helps your audience. As your channel grows, you'll have the opportunity to inspire, educate, and entertain a global audience while potentially earning income through various monetization methods.

21. Hosting Virtual Dance or Fitness Classes

Offering virtual dance or fitness classes is a great way to share your passion for dance or fitness while providing an accessible and convenient way for people to stay active and healthy. Here's how to get started:

21.1. Choose Your Niche and Style:

Determine the type of dance or fitness classes you want to offer. Consider your expertise and interests, whether it's Zumba, yoga, hip-hop dance, or another style.

21.2. Define Your Target Audience:

Identify the demographics and fitness levels of your potential students. This will help you tailor your classes to their needs.

21.3. Set Your Schedule:

Decide when you'll offer your virtual classes. Consider different time slots to accommodate various time zones.

21.4. Select a Platform:

Choose a platform for hosting your virtual classes. Popular options include Zoom, Skype, Microsoft Teams, or specialized fitness platforms like ZoomDance or FitGrid.

21.5. Equipment and Setup:

Gather the necessary equipment, such as a camera, microphone, and stable internet connection. Set up a dedicated space for your classes with proper lighting and sound.

21.6. Plan Your Classes:

Create a curriculum or lesson plan for your classes. Structure your classes with warm-ups, workouts, and cool-downs, ensuring they cater to different fitness levels.

21.7. Pricing and Payment:

Determine your pricing structure, whether it's per class, monthly subscriptions, or packages. Set up a secure payment system to collect fees.

21.8. Market Your Classes:

Promote your classes through social media, your website, email newsletters, and fitness or dance communities. Use eye-catching graphics and videos to showcase what participants can expect.

21.9. Offer Free Trials:

Consider offering free trial classes to attract new participants and give them a taste of your teaching style.

21.10. Engage with Participants:

Interact with your participants during classes, offer modifications for different fitness levels, and create a welcoming and encouraging atmosphere.

21.11. Record and Share:

Record your classes and make them available for participants who couldn't attend live or wish to revisit the content.

21.12. Feedback and Improvement:

Collect feedback from participants to continuously improve your classes. Use their suggestions to refine your teaching style and content.

21.13. Legal Considerations:

Ensure you have the necessary licenses or permissions to teach copyrighted dance routines or use copyrighted music. Consider liability insurance.

21.14. Safety First:

Emphasize safety during your classes. Encourage participants to consult with a healthcare professional before starting a new fitness routine.

21.15. Build a Community:

Create a sense of community among your participants. Consider setting up private groups or forums for discussions and support.

21.16. Adapt to Technology:

Stay informed about the latest virtual class technology and tools to enhance the quality of your classes.

Virtual dance or fitness classes offer a flexible and accessible way to share your expertise, connect with a global audience, and promote a healthy lifestyle. By delivering engaging and effective classes and building a strong online presence, you can create a successful and fulfilling career as a virtual dance or fitness instructor.

22. Virtual Assistance

Becoming a virtual assistant (VA) is an excellent way to offer administrative and support services to businesses and entrepreneurs while working remotely. Here's how to get started as a virtual assistant:

22.1. Determine Your Skills and Services:

Identify your strengths and the services you can provide. Common VA services include email management, scheduling, data entry, social media management, customer support, and more.

22.2. Create a Business Plan:

Develop a business plan outlining your services, target market, pricing structure, and business goals.

22.3. Legal Considerations:

Register your virtual assistant business, if necessary, and ensure you comply with local business regulations and tax laws.

22.4. Set Up a Home Office:

Create a dedicated and organized workspace at home. Ensure you have the necessary equipment, such as a computer, high-speed internet, and office software.

22.5. Build a Professional Website:

Create a professional website that showcases your services, skills, and client testimonials. Include a contact form for inquiries.

22.6. Establish a Strong Online Presence:

Create profiles on professional networking platforms like LinkedIn and freelancing websites like Upwork or Fiverr to attract potential clients.

22.7. Develop a Pricing Structure:

Determine your pricing strategy, whether it's hourly rates, project-based fees, or retainer packages. Research industry standards to set competitive prices.

22.8. Marketing and Networking:

Use social media, online communities, and networking events to market your services and connect with potential clients.

22.9. Create Contracts and Agreements:

Develop clear contracts and agreements that outline the scope of work, payment terms, deadlines, and confidentiality clauses for your clients.

22.10. Time Management:

Implement effective time management strategies to handle multiple clients and tasks efficiently.

22.11. Client Onboarding:

Establish a smooth onboarding process for new clients. Gather necessary information and expectations to provide high-quality service.

22.12. Use Productivity Tools:

Utilize productivity and project management tools such as Asana, Trello, or Slack to stay organized and collaborate with clients.

22.13. Communication Skills:

Maintain clear and professional communication with clients through email, phone calls, or video conferences.

22.14. Continuous Learning:

Stay updated on industry trends, tools, and software to offer the most valuable services to your clients.

22.15. Offer Exceptional Customer Service:

Provide excellent customer service to build trust and maintain long-term client relationships.

22.16. Evaluate Your Performance:

Regularly assess your performance and gather feedback from clients to make improvements.

22.17. Expand Your Services:

Consider expanding your skill set and offering additional services as your experience grows.

Virtual assistance offers flexibility, independence, and the opportunity to work with a diverse range of clients and industries. By providing efficient and reliable support services, you can establish a successful virtual assistant business and enjoy a fulfilling remote career.

23. Data Entry and Transcription

Data entry and transcription are popular online job opportunities that involve converting information from one format to another. Here's how to get started in these fields:

23.1. Assess Your Skills:

Determine if you have strong typing skills, attention to detail, and good listening skills (for transcription). These qualities are essential for data entry and transcription work.

23.2. Equipment and Software:

Ensure you have the necessary equipment, including a computer with reliable internet access and a comfortable workspace. You may also need transcription software and a good-quality headset if you're pursuing transcription work.

23.3. Develop Your Typing Speed:

Practice and improve your typing speed and accuracy. Faster typing will increase your productivity.

23.4. Choose a Specialization:

Decide whether you want to specialize in data entry, medical transcription, legal transcription, or general transcription. Each field has its unique requirements.

23.5. Training and Certification:

Consider enrolling in online courses or obtaining certifications to enhance your skills and credibility, especially for specialized transcription work.

23.6. Create a Professional Resume:

Develop a professional resume highlighting your data entry or transcription skills, training, and any relevant experience.

23.7. Find Job Opportunities:

Look for data entry or transcription job listings on job boards, freelancing platforms (e.g., Upwork, Freelancer), or specialized transcription websites.

23.8. Online Transcription Platforms:

Register on transcription platforms like Rev, TranscribeMe, or GoTranscript to access transcription job opportunities.

23.9. Set Up Payment Methods:

Set up a secure payment method, such as PayPal, to receive payments for your work.

23.10. Meet Deadlines:

Ensure you can meet project deadlines consistently, as timely delivery is crucial in these fields.

23.11. Protect Client Data:

Maintain strict confidentiality and data security protocols, especially when handling sensitive information.

23.12. Accuracy and Quality:

Focus on producing accurate and high-quality work. Transcripts, in particular, must be error-free and well-formatted.

23.13. Continuous Learning:

Stay updated on industry terminology, software, and transcription guidelines. Continuous learning is essential for staying competitive.

23.14. Build a Portfolio:

As you gain experience, create a portfolio showcasing your best work. This can help you attract more clients.

23.15. Network and Seek Reviews:

Network with professionals in your chosen field and encourage satisfied clients to leave positive reviews or referrals.

23.16. Pricing and Negotiation:

Set competitive rates for your services and be prepared to negotiate with clients, especially when starting out.

23.17. Be Reliable and Communicative:

Maintain clear communication with clients, and let them know if you encounter any issues that may affect deadlines.

Data entry and transcription can be excellent ways to earn income online, offering flexibility and the ability to work from home. However, they require attention to detail, dedication, and the ability to meet deadlines consistently.

With practice and commitment, you can build a successful career in these fields.

24. Online Bookkeeping

Online bookkeeping involves maintaining accurate financial records for businesses or individuals remotely. It's a valuable service, especially for small businesses and entrepreneurs. Here's how to start an online bookkeeping business:

24.1. Acquire the Necessary Skills and Knowledge:

Ensure you have a solid understanding of accounting principles, bookkeeping software (e.g., QuickBooks, Xero), and financial statements. Consider obtaining relevant certifications, such as a Certified Public Bookkeeper (CPB) credential.

24.2. Set Up Your Home Office:

Create a dedicated and organized workspace in your home, equipped with a computer, high-speed internet, accounting software, and other necessary tools.

24.3. Legal Structure and Licensing:

Decide on your business's legal structure (e.g., sole proprietorship, LLC) and register your business as required by local regulations. Check if you need any specific licenses or permits.

24.4. Choose Your Target Market:

Determine your ideal clients. This might include small businesses, freelancers, startups, or individuals who need bookkeeping services.

24.5. Develop Pricing Packages:

Establish pricing packages or hourly rates for your services. Consider offering different levels of bookkeeping services to cater to various client needs.

24.6. Create a Professional Website:

Build a professional website that showcases your services, pricing, qualifications, and contact information. Ensure your website is user-friendly and mobile-responsive.

24.7. Marketing and Networking:

Market your bookkeeping services through social media, local business networks, and online communities. Consider running targeted online ads.

24.8. Client Contracts:

Create clear and comprehensive client contracts that outline the scope of work, fees, payment terms, and confidentiality agreements.

24.9. Bookkeeping Software:

Familiarize yourself with popular bookkeeping software and choose the one that best suits your needs and the needs of your clients.

24.10. Data Security:

Implement robust data security measures to protect your clients' sensitive financial information.

24.11. Offer Virtual Consultations:

Provide virtual consultations to potential clients to discuss their needs and determine how you can help them.

24.12. Set Up Accounting Systems:

Establish accounting systems and processes for your clients, including data entry, reconciliations, payroll, and financial reporting.

24.13. Stay Informed and Updated:

Keep up with changes in tax laws and accounting regulations that may affect your clients' financial records.

24.14. Professionalism and Communication:

Maintain professionalism in your interactions with clients. Ensure clear and timely communication.

24.15. Continuous Learning:

Pursue ongoing education and training in accounting and bookkeeping to stay competitive and offer valuable services.

24.16. Client Relationships:

Build strong relationships with your clients by providing accurate, reliable, and timely bookkeeping services.

24.17. Bookkeeping Associations:

Consider joining bookkeeping associations or organizations that can provide support, resources, and networking opportunities.

Online bookkeeping offers the convenience of remote work and a high demand for skilled professionals. By providing accurate financial management and maintaining excellent client relationships, you can build a successful online bookkeeping business that serves the financial needs of businesses and individuals.

25. Graphic Design (Basic Skills)

Graphic design involves creating visual content for various purposes, including branding, marketing, and communication. If you're interested in starting a career in graphic design, here are the fundamental steps to begin:

25.1. Develop Your Creative Skills:

Start by honing your creative skills and exploring your artistic talents. Experiment with different design elements such as colors, typography, and layout.

25.2. Acquire the Necessary Tools:

Invest in essential graphic design tools such as a computer with design software (Adobe Creative Suite, Canva, or similar), a graphics tablet, and a good-quality monitor.

25.3. Learn Graphic Design Basics:

Study the fundamental principles of graphic design, including composition, balance, contrast, hierarchy, and color theory. There are numerous online tutorials and courses available.

25.4. Get Design Software Proficiency:

Familiarize yourself with industry-standard graphic design software like

Adobe Photoshop, Illustrator, and InDesign. Practice using these tools to create designs.

25.5. Study Typography:

Typography is a critical aspect of graphic design. Learn about different fonts, typefaces, and how to use text effectively in design projects.

25.6. Understand Color Theory:

Explore the principles of color theory, including color harmonies, contrasts, and the psychology of color. This knowledge is essential for creating visually appealing designs.

25.7. Develop Your Portfolio:

Start building a portfolio of your design work. Include a variety of projects that showcase your skills and style. Your portfolio is crucial for attracting clients or employers.

25.8. Practice Consistently:

Regular practice is essential for improving your design skills. Challenge yourself with design exercises and personal projects.

25.9. Learn Basic Design Principles:

Understand essential design principles, such as alignment, proximity, repetition, and contrast, to create visually cohesive designs.

25.10. Stay Inspired:

Follow design trends and stay inspired by browsing design websites, magazines, and social media platforms. Attend design conferences or webinars for further inspiration.

25.11. Study Design History:

Familiarize yourself with the history of graphic design and famous designers. Understanding design history can provide valuable insights into the evolution of design styles.

25.12. Networking and Feedback:

Join online design communities, forums, and social media groups to connect with other designers. Seek feedback on your work to improve.

25.13. Freelance or Entry-Level Work:

Consider freelancing or seeking entry-level positions at design agencies, marketing firms, or businesses to gain practical experience and build your resume.

25.14. Set Up Your Online Presence:

Create a professional website or online portfolio to showcase your work and make it easy for potential clients or employers to find you.

25.15. Offer Pro Bono Work:

Initially, consider offering pro bono design services to build your portfolio and gain experience. Non-profit organizations often appreciate free design help.

25.16. Build a Personal Brand:

Develop your personal brand as a designer. Your unique style and reputation can help you stand out in a competitive field.

25.17. Continuous Learning:

Graphic design is an evolving field. Stay updated on new design trends, software updates, and techniques through online courses, workshops, and design books.

Starting a career in graphic design requires dedication, creativity, and continuous learning. Building a strong portfolio and establishing a unique style are essential steps to attract clients or employers. With persistence and passion, you can develop your graphic design skills and succeed in this exciting field.

26. Social Media Management (Basic Skills)

Social media management involves creating, curating, and posting content on social media platforms to engage an audience and achieve specific marketing goals. If you're interested in becoming a social media manager, here are the basic steps to get started:

26.1. Understand Social Media Platforms:

Familiarize yourself with popular social media platforms such as Facebook, Instagram, Twitter, LinkedIn, Pinterest, and TikTok. Understand their unique features, audience demographics, and best practices.

26.2. Develop Strong Communication Skills:

Effective communication is crucial for social media management. Improve your writing, editing, and interpersonal skills to create compelling content and engage with followers.

26.3. Identify Your Niche:

Decide on a niche or industry you're passionate about or knowledgeable in. Specializing in a particular niche can make you more appealing to potential clients.

26.4. Create Professional Profiles:

Set up professional social media profiles for yourself on platforms like LinkedIn and Twitter to showcase your expertise and connect with industry professionals.

26.5. Stay Informed About Trends:

Stay updated on current social media trends, algorithm changes, and emerging platforms by following industry news and attending webinars or conferences.

26.6. Use Social Media Management Tools:

Learn how to use social media management tools like Hootsuite, Buffer, or Sprout Social to schedule posts, track analytics, and manage multiple accounts efficiently.

26.7. Build Your Personal Brand:

Establish your personal brand as a social media manager. Showcase your skills, experience, and success stories to build credibility.

26.8. Create a Portfolio:

Compile a portfolio of your work, including sample social media posts, graphics, and analytics reports. A portfolio demonstrates your abilities to potential clients or employers.

26.9. Offer Your Services:

Start offering social media management services to individuals, small businesses, or non-profit organizations in your network. Offer competitive rates to attract your first clients.

26.10. Plan Content Strategy:

Develop content strategies for your clients, including content calendars, post schedules, and ideas for engaging and shareable content.

26.11. Content Creation Skills:

Improve your skills in content creation, including graphic design, photography, and video editing. High-quality visuals can significantly impact social media success.

26.12. Track and Analyze Performance:

Learn how to use social media analytics tools to track the performance of your posts and campaigns. Analyze data to make data-driven decisions.

26.13. Engage and Interact:

Actively engage with your clients' followers by responding to comments, messages, and inquiries. Building a sense of community is crucial for social media success.

26.14. Crisis Management:

Be prepared to handle social media crises and negative comments professionally and swiftly.

26.15. Continuous Learning:

Stay updated on changes in social media algorithms, advertising options, and best practices through online courses and industry resources.

26.16. Legal and Ethical Considerations:

Familiarize yourself with legal and ethical guidelines related to social media marketing, including privacy and advertising regulations.

26.17. Report and Evaluate:

Regularly provide clients with performance reports and insights. Use data to optimize social media strategies and achieve better results.

Social media management can be a dynamic and rewarding career path. By building your skills, establishing a strong online presence, and delivering results for clients, you can develop a successful social media management business or secure employment in this growing field.

27. Virtual Event Planning

Virtual event planning involves organizing and managing online events, conferences, webinars, workshops, and virtual meetings. As the demand for virtual events continues to grow, here are the steps to get started in this field:

27.1. Understand Virtual Events:

Familiarize yourself with the concept of virtual events and the various types of online gatherings, including webinars, virtual conferences, product launches, and online workshops.

27.2. Develop Event Planning Skills:

Hone your event planning skills, which include project management, time management, communication, and attention to detail.

27.3. Choose a Niche:

Decide on a niche or type of virtual event you want to specialize in, such as corporate meetings, educational webinars, or social gatherings.

27.4. Study Online Platforms:

Research and become proficient in virtual event platforms and tools like Zoom, Microsoft Teams, Webex, and event management software like Eventbrite or Cvent.

27.5. Build a Network:

Connect with industry professionals, speakers, vendors, and potential clients in the virtual event space. Networking can help you find opportunities and partnerships.

27.6. Legal Considerations:

Understand legal considerations related to virtual events, such as contracts, copyright issues, and compliance with data protection regulations.

27.7. Create a Business Plan:

Develop a comprehensive business plan that outlines your services, pricing, target market, and marketing strategies.

27.8. Offer Virtual Event Services:

Start offering your virtual event planning services to clients or organizations in your network. Showcase your expertise and professionalism.

27.9. Marketing and Promotion:

Market your services through your website, social media, email marketing, and online advertising. Highlight your experience in organizing successful virtual events.

27.10. Develop Event Proposals:

Create event proposals that include event goals, budget estimates, event agenda, and details about speakers or presenters.

27.11. Event Technology:

Stay updated on the latest event technology trends and tools to enhance the virtual event experience.

27.12. Design Engaging Content:

Collaborate with speakers, presenters, and content creators to develop engaging presentations, workshops, or webinars.

27.13. Technical Support:

Be prepared to offer technical support to participants during virtual events, such as troubleshooting audio or video issues.

27.14. Rehearsals and Run-Throughs:

Conduct rehearsals and run-throughs with event presenters to ensure everything runs smoothly during the live event.

27.15. Monitor and Engage:

During the event, actively monitor participant engagement, answer questions, and manage technical hiccups in real-time.

27.16. Post-Event Analysis:

Conduct post-event surveys and gather feedback from participants to evaluate the event's success and identify areas for improvement.

27.17. Continuous Learning:

Stay informed about industry trends, new virtual event technologies, and best practices through webinars, courses, and industry publications.

Virtual event planning offers opportunities to create engaging and impactful online experiences for clients and participants. By mastering the technical aspects of virtual events and providing exceptional service, you can establish yourself as a trusted virtual event planner in a growing industry.

28. Rent Out Your Property on Airbnb

Renting out your property on Airbnb can be a lucrative way to earn income from your home or investment property. Here's how to get started:

28.1. Legal and Regulatory Compliance:

Research local laws and regulations regarding short-term rentals in your area. Ensure you have any necessary permits or licenses.

28.2. Prepare Your Property:

Clean, declutter, and furnish your property to make it appealing to potential guests. Consider investing in quality amenities and furniture.

28.3. Take High-Quality Photos:

Invest in professional photography or take high-quality photos that showcase your property's features, including bedrooms, common areas, and outdoor spaces.

28.4. Create an Airbnb Listing:

Sign up for an Airbnb host account and create a detailed and engaging listing. Include a catchy title, a comprehensive description, and clear house rules.

28.5. Set Pricing and Availability:

Determine your nightly rates based on factors like location, property type, and local demand. Use Airbnb's pricing tools to help set competitive rates.

28.6. Create House Rules:

Establish clear and reasonable house rules that guests must follow, covering topics like check-in/check-out times, smoking policies, and pet rules.

28.7. Verify Your Identity:

Complete Airbnb's identity verification process, which can enhance trust among potential guests.

28.8. Communication and Availability:

Be responsive to guest inquiries and messages. Maintain open and timely communication with guests.

28.9. Offer Amenities:

Provide essential amenities such as clean bedding, towels, toiletries, and a well-equipped kitchen. Consider extras like Wi-Fi, Netflix, or a hot tub.

28.10. Consider Safety Measures:

Install smoke detectors, fire extinguishers, and carbon monoxide detectors. Ensure your property is secure with reliable locks and security measures.

28.11. Manage Your Calendar:

Keep your Airbnb calendar up to date to accurately reflect availability and avoid double bookings.

28.12. Check Local Tax Requirements:

Research if you're required to collect and remit local taxes on Airbnb bookings. Airbnb may provide tools to assist with tax compliance.

28.13. Guest Screening:

Carefully review guest inquiries and profiles. Consider implementing guest verification requirements for added security.

28.14. Hosting Responsibilities:

Be available for guest check-in or provide clear self-check-in instructions. Offer assistance during your guests' stay and be ready to address any issues promptly.

28.15. Housekeeping and Maintenance:

Maintain your property's cleanliness and perform regular maintenance tasks to ensure a comfortable stay for guests.

28.16. Leave a Guest Guidebook:

Create a guidebook with local recommendations, emergency contacts, and instructions for using appliances and amenities in your property.

28.17. Reviews and Feedback:

Encourage guests to leave reviews after their stay, and respond to reviews in a polite and professional manner. Positive reviews can boost your listing's visibility.

28.18. Continuous Improvement:

Continuously improve your property based on guest feedback and market trends. Consider upgrading amenities or making renovations when necessary.

28.19. Prepare for Emergencies:

Develop a plan for handling emergencies such as power outages, plumbing issues, or security concerns.

Renting out your property on Airbnb can be a rewarding source of income, but it also requires dedication and attention to detail. By providing an exceptional guest experience and adhering to best practices, you can attract more bookings and build a successful Airbnb hosting business.

29. Car Sharing and Ridesharing

Car sharing and ridesharing platforms like Uber, Lyft, and Airbnb's Turo allow you to earn money by offering transportation services or renting out your vehicle. Here's how to get started:

29.1. Vehicle Requirements:

Ensure your vehicle meets the requirements of the car sharing or ridesharing platform you choose. These requirements typically include age, model, and condition.

29.2. Driver's License and Insurance:

Make sure you have a valid driver's license and appropriate auto insurance coverage. Some platforms may require specific insurance policies for ridesharing.

29.3. Choose a Platform:

Decide whether you want to offer ridesharing services as a driver (e.g., Uber, Lyft) or rent out your vehicle (e.g., Turo, Getaround).

29.4. Sign Up:

Create an account on your chosen platform. You'll need to provide personal information, vehicle details, and documentation.

29.5. Background Check:

Expect to undergo a background check, including a driving record check and criminal background check for rideshare services.

29.6. Vehicle Maintenance:

Keep your vehicle well-maintained to ensure it's safe and in good working condition. Regularly service and clean it.

29.7. Pricing and Availability:

Set competitive pricing for your rideshare services or vehicle rental. Adjust your rates based on factors like demand and location.

29.8. Safety Measures:

Implement safety measures such as providing hand sanitizers and face masks for passengers during the COVID-19 pandemic. Also, adhere to safety guidelines provided by the platform.

29.9. Communication:

Maintain clear and prompt communication with passengers or renters. Answer inquiries, provide directions, and confirm bookings.

29.10. Ratings and Reviews:

Focus on providing excellent service to earn positive ratings and reviews, which can increase your chances of getting more bookings.

29.11. Taxes and Income Reporting:

Keep track of your earnings and expenses for tax purposes. Depending on your location, you may need to report your income and pay taxes on it.

29.12. Ride Sharing as a Driver:

If you're a rideshare driver, consider driving during peak hours or in areas with high demand to maximize your earnings.

29.13. Vehicle Rental Guidelines:

If you're renting out your vehicle, set clear guidelines for renters, including pick-up and drop-off procedures, fuel requirements, and cleaning expectations.

29.14. Safety and Security:

Take safety precautions during rideshare services, such as verifying the passenger's identity and ensuring the vehicle is in good condition.

29.15. Record Keeping:

Maintain records of all transactions, bookings, and expenses associated with your car sharing or ridesharing activities.

29.16. Customer Service:

Provide excellent customer service and be responsive to inquiries, concerns, or issues that may arise during bookings.

29.17. Continuous Learning:

Stay updated on any changes to the platform's policies, fees, or safety regulations. Attend training or webinars provided by the platform if available.

Car sharing and ridesharing can be flexible ways to earn money with your vehicle. However, it's essential to prioritize safety, maintain a good reputation, and adhere to platform rules and regulations to ensure a successful and profitable experience.

30. Rent Out Your Parking Space

Renting out your parking space, whether it's a driveway, garage, or parking spot, can be an excellent way to generate income. Here's how to get started:

30.1. Check Local Regulations:

First, research your local zoning and parking regulations to ensure you're allowed to rent out your parking space. Some areas may have restrictions or requirements.

30.2. Prepare the Space:

Make sure your parking space is clean, well-maintained, and safe for vehicles.

Clear any debris, repair any damage, and consider adding lighting if necessary.

30.3. Determine Availability:

Decide when your parking space is available for rent. You can offer it on a regular basis, for special events, or during specific hours.

30.4. Pricing Strategy:

Set a competitive price for your parking space based on factors like location, demand, and convenience. Research similar listings in your area to determine an appropriate rate.

30.5. Take Photos:

Capture clear photos of your parking space, showcasing its accessibility and any unique features. High-quality images can attract renters.

30.6. Create a Listing:

Sign up on a parking space rental platform like JustPark, SpotHero, or Airbnb (if they offer parking space listings) and create a detailed listing for your space.

30.7. Description and Amenities:

Write a comprehensive description of your parking space, including any amenities like security features or proximity to popular destinations.

30.8. Availability Calendar:

Keep your availability calendar up to date to prevent double bookings and ensure a smooth rental process.

30.9. House Rules:

Set clear rules for renters, including instructions for entering and leaving the parking space, any restrictions, and policies on cleanliness and behavior.

30.10. Communication:

Be responsive to inquiries from potential renters and provide clear instructions for accessing the parking space.

30.11. Security Measures:

Consider installing security cameras or lighting to enhance the safety of your parking space and provide peace of mind to renters.

30.12. Legal Considerations:

Draft a rental agreement that outlines the terms and conditions of parking space rental, including payment, liability, and any rules renters must follow.

30.13. Payment Methods:

Set up a secure and convenient payment method for renters. Online payment platforms or mobile apps can simplify the payment process.

30.14. Insurance:

Check with your insurance provider to understand how renting out your parking space may affect your coverage. You may need additional liability coverage.

30.15. Maintenance:

Regularly inspect and maintain your parking space to ensure it remains in good condition and safe for renters.

30.16. Marketing and Promotion:

Promote your parking space through social media, local classifieds, and online parking space rental platforms to attract renters.

30.17. Guest Feedback:

Encourage renters to leave feedback and reviews after using your parking space. Positive reviews can boost your space's reputation.

30.18. Continuous Improvement:

Continuously assess the rental process and consider making improvements based on renter feedback and market demand.

Renting out your parking space can be a convenient and passive source of income. By providing a safe, well-maintained space and adhering to legal and safety considerations, you can attract regular renters and generate consistent income.

31. Renting Photography Equipment

Renting out photography equipment can be a lucrative business, especially if you have a collection of high-quality gear. Here's how to get started:

31.1. Inventory Assessment:

Take an inventory of the photography equipment you have available for rent. Ensure that all equipment is in good working condition and well-maintained.

31.2. Pricing and Rates:

Research the market to determine competitive pricing for your equipment rentals. Consider offering daily, weekly, and monthly rental rates.

31.3. Rental Terms and Policies:

Draft clear rental terms and policies that cover issues like security deposits, insurance requirements, rental duration, late fees, and damage or loss charges.

31.4. Legal Considerations:

Consult with a legal expert to create rental agreements that protect your equipment and outline the responsibilities of both parties.

31.5. Insurance:

Ensure that your equipment is adequately insured. Renters may need to provide proof of insurance or pay for additional coverage when renting high-value equipment.

31.6. Online Presence:

Create a professional website or list your equipment on established photography equipment rental platforms. Include high-quality photos and detailed descriptions of each item.

31.7. Payment Processing:

Set up a secure payment processing system to accept rental payments online. PayPal and Stripe are popular options.

31.8. Rental Scheduling:

Implement a booking system or calendar on your website to manage equipment reservations and availability.

31.9. Cleaning and Maintenance:

Regularly clean and maintain your equipment to ensure it's in optimal condition for renters.

31.10. Security Measures:

Establish security procedures to verify the identity of renters and reduce the risk of theft or damage to your equipment.

31.11. Rental Pick-Up and Drop-Off:

Determine how equipment will be exchanged between you and renters. Consider local pick-up and drop-off options or shipping methods.

31.12. Customer Service:

Provide excellent customer service by being responsive to inquiries, offering technical support, and addressing any issues promptly.

31.13. Marketing and Promotion:

Promote your equipment rental business through photography forums, social media, local photography clubs, and partnerships with photography schools or studios.

31.14. Feedback and Reviews:

Encourage renters to leave feedback and reviews after using your equipment. Positive reviews can build trust and attract more renters.

31.15. Continuous Expansion:

Consider expanding your equipment inventory based on market demand and trends in photography. Stay up to date with the latest equipment releases.

31.16. Safety and Security:

Implement safety measures to protect your equipment during rentals, such as requiring renters to sign for equipment upon receipt.

31.17. Rental Periods:

Be flexible with rental periods to accommodate various photography projects, from short-term events to long-term projects.

Renting out photography equipment can be a profitable venture, especially if you have specialized gear that is in demand. By providing reliable and well-maintained equipment, along with exceptional customer service, you can establish a successful photography equipment rental business.

32. Stock Market Investing (Basic)

Investing in the stock market can be an effective way to build wealth over time. Here are some basic steps to get started with stock market investing:

32.1. Education and Research:

Begin by educating yourself about the stock market and how it works. Read books, articles, and websites on investing and follow financial news.

32.2. Set Clear Goals:

Determine your financial goals and the purpose of your investments. Are you saving for retirement, a major purchase, or simply growing your wealth?

32.3. Assess Risk Tolerance:

Understand your risk tolerance. How comfortable are you with the possibility of losing some or all of your investment? This will help you determine your investment strategy.

32.4. Emergency Fund:

Before investing, ensure you have an emergency fund with enough money to cover at least three to six months' worth of living expenses.

32.5. Pay Off High-Interest Debt:

If you have high-interest debts, like credit card balances, it's often a better financial move to pay those off before investing.

32.6. Choose an Investment Account:

Open an investment account, such as an individual brokerage account or an individual retirement account (IRA), depending on your goals.

32.7. Diversification:

Diversify your investments by spreading your money across different asset classes (stocks, bonds, real estate) to reduce risk.

32.8. Investment Horizon:

Determine your investment horizon, which is the length of time you plan to hold your investments. Long-term investments generally have higher growth potential.

32.9. Selecting Stocks:

Research and choose individual stocks or exchange-traded funds (ETFs) that align with your investment goals and risk tolerance.

32.10. Dollar-Cost Averaging:

Consider using a dollar-cost averaging strategy, where you invest a fixed amount of money at regular intervals (e.g., monthly) regardless of market conditions.

32.11. Keep Costs Low:

Pay attention to fees and expenses associated with your investments. Look for low-cost index funds or ETFs with low expense ratios.

32.12. Monitor Your Investments:

Regularly review your portfolio to ensure it aligns with your goals and risk tolerance. Rebalance if necessary.

32.13. Avoid Emotional Decisions:

Emotions can lead to impulsive decisions. Stick to your investment strategy and avoid making drastic changes based on market fluctuations.

32.14. Long-Term Perspective:

Understand that stock market investing is typically a long-term endeavor. Short-term volatility is common, but over time, the market tends to grow.

32.15. Continue Learning:

Stay informed about financial markets and investment opportunities. Consider taking courses or seeking advice from financial professionals.

32.16. Tax Considerations:

Be aware of the tax implications of your investments. Consult with a tax advisor to optimize your tax strategy.

32.17. Start Small:

You don't need a large sum of money to start investing. Many brokerage platforms offer no or low minimum investment requirements.

Remember that investing in the stock market carries risks, and there are no guarantees of profit. It's important to start with a solid foundation of knowledge, set clear goals, and develop a disciplined approach to managing your investments. Over time, consistent investing and patience can lead to financial growth and security.

33. Cryptocurrency Trading (Basic)

Cryptocurrency trading can be a rewarding but volatile endeavor. Here are some basic steps to get started with cryptocurrency trading:

33.1. Education and Research:

Begin by educating yourself about cryptocurrencies and blockchain technology. Understand the fundamentals, such as how blockchain works, what different cryptocurrencies are, and the technology behind them.

33.2. Choose a Reliable Exchange:

Select a reputable cryptocurrency exchange platform where you can buy, sell, and trade cryptocurrencies. Research and compare different exchanges based on fees, security features, available coins, and user reviews.

33.3. Set Up a Wallet:

Secure a cryptocurrency wallet to store your assets safely. Consider using hardware wallets or software wallets with strong security features.

33.4. Start with Bitcoin:

If you're new to cryptocurrency, start with Bitcoin (BTC). It's the most established and widely recognized cryptocurrency.

33.5. Develop a Trading Plan:

Create a clear trading plan that outlines your goals, risk tolerance, and strategies. Decide on your entry and exit points and establish stop-loss orders to limit potential losses.

33.6. Risk Management:

Never invest more than you can afford to lose. Cryptocurrency markets are highly volatile, and prices can change rapidly.

33.7. Start Small:

Begin with a small amount of capital to gain experience and confidence. As you become more comfortable, you can gradually increase your investments.

33.8. Technical Analysis:

Learn about technical analysis, which involves analyzing price charts and patterns to make informed trading decisions.

33.9. Fundamental Analysis:

Understand fundamental analysis, which involves evaluating the underlying technology, adoption, and use cases of cryptocurrencies.

33.10. Stay Informed:

Stay up to date with cryptocurrency news and market trends. Follow influential figures and news sources in the crypto space.

33.11. Security Measures:

Implement strong security measures to protect your investments. Use two-factor authentication (2FA) and consider enabling other security features provided by your exchange.

33.12. Trading Pairs:

Understand trading pairs, which represent the exchange rate between two cryptocurrencies. For example, BTC/USD represents the Bitcoin-to-US Dollar trading pair.

33.13. Limit Orders and Market Orders:

Learn how to place limit orders (buy or sell at a specific price) and market orders (buy or sell at the current market price).

33.14. Practice with Demo Accounts:

Some exchanges offer demo accounts where you can practice trading with virtual funds before using real money.

33.15. Start Trading:

Once you're comfortable, start making small trades and gain experience. Keep a trading journal to track your decisions and outcomes.

33.16. Taxes and Reporting:

Understand the tax implications of crypto currency trading in your country. Keep accurate records of your trades for tax reporting purposes.

33.17. Be Cautious of Scams:

Be cautious of crypto currency scams and phishing attempts. Always verify the legitimacy of websites and emails before sharing sensitive information.

33.18. Continuous Learning:

Crypto currency markets are dynamic and ever-evolving. Stay curious and keep learning about new projects, technologies, and trends in the crypto space.

Crypto currency trading can be profitable, but it's also risky and requires a thorough understanding of the market. Start with caution, take the time to learn, and consider seeking advice from experienced traders or financial professionals.

34. Peer-to-Peer Lending

Peer-to-peer (P2P) lending, also known as person-to-person lending, is a method of borrowing and lending money directly between individuals or "peers" without traditional financial institutions like banks. Here's how to get started with P2P lending:

34.1. Understand the Concept:

Familiarize yourself with the P2P lending concept. It involves individuals lending money to others in exchange for interest payments.

34.2. Choose a P2P Platform:

Research and select a reputable P2P lending platform. Some well-known platforms include LendingClub, Prosper, and Funding Circle.

34.3. Create an Account:

Sign up for an account on your chosen P2P lending platform. You may need to provide personal information and financial details.

34.4. Verify Your Identity:

Complete identity verification processes required by the platform, which typically include providing identification documents.

34.5. Assess Risk Tolerance:

Determine your risk tolerance and investment goals. P2P lending involves some level of risk, including the potential for loan defaults.

34.6. Diversification:

Spread your investments across multiple loans to reduce risk. Diversification can help mitigate the impact of individual loan defaults.

34.7. Choose Your Investment Strategy:

Decide whether you want to invest in consumer loans, small business loans, or other loan types. Each has its own risk profile and potential returns.

34.8. Review Borrower Profiles:

Carefully review borrower profiles on the platform. Look at factors like credit score, employment history, and loan purpose to assess creditworthiness.

34.9. Invest:

Invest in loans that align with your investment strategy. You can typically choose the loans you want to fund based on borrower profiles.

34.10. Loan Terms:

Understand the loan terms, including interest rates, loan duration, and repayment schedules. Different loans offer various interest rates and durations.

34.11. Monitor Your Investments:

Keep track of your loan investments and monitor borrower repayments. Some platforms provide tools for tracking your portfolio.

34.12. Reinvestment:

Reinvest the repayments you receive into new loans to keep your money working for you.

34.13. Risk Assessment:

Be aware that there is a risk of loan defaults, and not all borrowers may repay their loans. Factor this into your investment strategy.

34.14. Withdraw Funds:

Most P2P lending platforms allow you to withdraw your earnings at any time. You can transfer funds back to your bank account or reinvest them.

34.15. Tax Considerations:

Understand the tax implications of P2P lending income in your country. It may be subject to taxation.

34.16. Due Diligence:

Continuously conduct due diligence on the P2P platform itself. Ensure it complies with regulations and maintains transparency.

34.17. Stay Informed:

Stay informed about changes in the P2P lending industry, platform updates, and any regulatory developments.

P2P lending can be an alternative investment strategy that potentially offers attractive returns compared to traditional savings accounts or bonds. However, it's important to be aware of the risks involved and to diversify your investments to minimize potential losses. Regularly monitoring your investments and conducting thorough due diligence on borrowers and platforms are key to success in P2P lending.

35. Online Real Estate Investing

Online real estate investing allows you to invest in real estate properties without the need to buy physical properties. Here are steps to get started:

35.1. Understand Online Real Estate Investing:

Familiarize yourself with the concept of online real estate investing. It involves investing in real estate properties through online platforms or real estate investment trusts (REITs).

35.2. Research Online Real Estate Platforms:

Research and choose an online real estate platform that aligns with your investment goals. Popular platforms include Fundrise, RealtyMogul, and CrowdStreet.

35.3. Create an Account:

Sign up for an account on your chosen online real estate platform. Provide necessary information and complete identity verification.

35.4. Assess Your Investment Goals:

Determine your investment objectives, such as income generation, capital appreciation, or diversification.

35.5. Choose an Investment Strategy:

Decide on your investment strategy, whether it's investing in commercial real estate, residential properties, or other real estate assets.

35.6. Review Property Offerings:

Explore the real estate properties available for investment on the platform. Examine property details, location, expected returns, and risk factors.

35.7. Diversification:

Diversify your investments by spreading your capital across multiple properties to reduce risk.

35.8. Investment Amount:

Decide how much you want to invest in each property or REIT. Most platforms have minimum investment requirements.

35.9. Fund Your Account:

Transfer funds to your online real estate investment account to begin investing.

35.10. Monitor Investments:

Keep track of your real estate investments through the platform's dashboard. Monitor property performance, rental income, and returns.

35.11. Reinvestment or Withdrawal:

Decide whether you want to reinvest your earnings into additional properties or withdraw funds to your bank account.

35.12. Tax Considerations:

Be aware of the tax implications of online real estate investing in your country. Real estate income may be subject to taxation.

35.13. Due Diligence:

Conduct due diligence on the real estate platform, including reviewing its track record, fees, and compliance with regulations.

35.14. Stay Informed:

Stay informed about market trends, property updates, and any changes in the real estate industry that may affect your investments.

35.15. Risk Management:

Understand the risks associated with online real estate investing, such as property market fluctuations and potential liquidity constraints.

35.16. Long-Term Perspective:

Online real estate investing often involves longer investment horizons. Be patient and maintain a long-term perspective.

Online real estate investing provides an opportunity to diversify your investment portfolio with real estate assets without the responsibilities of property management. However, it's essential to thoroughly research and understand the platform and properties you invest in and consider the risks involved in real estate markets.

36. Virtual Receptionist Services

Virtual receptionist services provide remote reception and administrative support to businesses, often through a team of virtual assistants. If you're interested in offering virtual receptionist services, here are the steps to get started:

36.1. Define Your Services:

Determine the scope of services you'll offer as a virtual receptionist. Common services include answering calls, managing appointments, handling inquiries, and providing customer support.

36.2. Legal Considerations:

Establish your business structure (e.g., sole proprietorship, LLC) and comply with any local or industry-specific regulations. Consult with a legal expert if necessary.

36.3. Business Plan:

Create a business plan outlining your services, pricing structure, target market, and marketing strategies.

36.4. Develop Your Skills:

Hone your communication skills, phone etiquette, and organizational abilities. Virtual receptionists must be professional and efficient in managing client interactions.

36.5. Technology Setup:

Invest in the necessary technology, including a reliable phone system, computer, internet connection, and software for managing appointments and tasks.

36.6. Virtual Assistant Training:

Train any virtual assistants or team members you plan to work with. Ensure they understand your clients' needs and can provide exceptional service.

36.7. Pricing Structure:

Decide on your pricing structure, whether it's per-call, hourly, or based on the number of services provided. Consider competitive rates in the industry.

36.8. Marketing and Promotion:

Create a professional website and use digital marketing strategies to promote your virtual receptionist services. Highlight your professionalism and reliability.

36.9. Service Agreements:

Develop clear service agreements or contracts that outline the terms and conditions of your virtual receptionist services, including confidentiality agreements.

36.10. Client Onboarding:

Develop an onboarding process for new clients. Gather information about their business needs, communication preferences, and specific requirements.

36.11. Set Up Communication Channels:

Implement communication channels such as phone lines, email, and messaging platforms to provide seamless support to your clients.

36.12. Appointment Scheduling Tools:

Use appointment scheduling software to efficiently manage clients' schedules and reminders.

36.13. Security Measures:

Implement robust security measures to protect client data and ensure confidentiality.

36.14. Customer Support:

Provide excellent customer support to clients and their customers. Be responsive and professional in handling inquiries and requests.

36.15. Continuous Learning:

Stay updated on industry trends, customer service best practices, and technology advancements that can improve your virtual receptionist services.

36.16. Feedback and Improvement:

Collect feedback from clients to continually improve your services. Make adjustments based on client suggestions and evolving business needs.

36.17. 24/7 Availability (Optional):

Consider offering 24/7 virtual receptionist services to accommodate clients with round-the-clock needs.

Virtual receptionist services can be a valuable asset to businesses looking to enhance their customer service and administrative support without the cost of hiring in-house staff. By providing professional and reliable service, you can build a loyal client base and establish a successful virtual receptionist business.

37. Online Data Entry

Online data entry is a remote job that involves entering, managing, and organizing data into digital formats. Here's how to get started with online data entry:

37.1. Assess Your Skills:

Evaluate your typing speed, accuracy, and proficiency with data entry software and tools. Online data entry requires attention to detail.

37.2. Acquire Necessary Equipment:

Ensure you have a computer with a reliable internet connection and necessary software for data entry tasks.

37.3. Set Up a Workspace:

Create a quiet and organized workspace where you can focus on data entry tasks without distractions.

37.4. Identify Data Entry Opportunities:

Look for online platforms, job boards, and freelancing websites that offer data entry jobs. Some popular platforms include Upwork, Freelancer, and Fiverr.

37.5. Create a Professional Profile:

If you're using freelancing platforms, create a professional profile that highlights your data entry skills, experience, and qualifications.

37.6. Search for Jobs:

Browse data entry job listings and apply to positions that match your skills and interests. Pay attention to project details, deadlines, and payment terms.

37.7. Networking:

Connect with others in the data entry field on professional networks like LinkedIn. Networking can lead to job opportunities.

37.8. Skill Development:

If you're looking to improve your data entry skills, consider taking online courses or tutorials to learn about specific data entry software or techniques.

37.9. Prepare Sample Work:

Create a portfolio of sample data entry projects to showcase your skills to potential clients or employers.

37.10. Time Management:

Manage your time effectively to meet project deadlines and maintain a good reputation as a reliable data entry professional.

37.11. Accuracy and Quality:

Focus on accuracy and quality in your work. Double-check data for errors and inconsistencies before submission.

37.12. Communication:

Maintain open and clear communication with clients or employers to ensure you understand project requirements and expectations.

37.13. Data Security:

Be aware of data security and confidentiality. Follow best practices for handling sensitive information if it's part of your job.

37.14. Payment and Invoicing:

Set up a payment system or use freelancing platform features to receive payments for your data entry work. Ensure you invoice clients promptly.

37.15. Continuous Learning:

Stay updated on data entry software and industry trends to remain competitive in the field.

37.16. Client Feedback:

Encourage clients to provide feedback and reviews after completing projects. Positive feedback can enhance your reputation.

37.17. Expand Your Skills (Optional):

Consider diversifying your skill set by learning related skills like spreadsheet management or transcription.

Online data entry can be a flexible way to earn income from the comfort of your home. By honing your skills, delivering high-quality work, and effectively managing your freelance career, you can build a successful online data entry business or career.

38. Email Management

Email management involves organizing, prioritizing, and responding to emails efficiently. Whether you're handling your own emails or offering email management services, these steps can help streamline the process:

38.1. Use a Dedicated Email Address:

Create a professional and dedicated email address for managing work-related emails, separate from personal emails.

38.2. Email Software or Client:

Use an email software or client that suits your needs. Popular options include Gmail, Outlook, and Thunderbird.

38.3. Organize Your Inbox:

Set up folders, labels, or categories to organize your emails. Create folders for different projects, clients, or categories to keep your inbox clutter-free.

38.4. Unsubscribe and Filters:

Unsubscribe from unnecessary newsletters and promotional emails. Use email filters to automatically sort emails into relevant folders.

38.5. Prioritize Emails:

Prioritize emails based on urgency and importance. Use labels or flags to mark emails that require immediate attention.

38.6. Email Etiquette:

Follow professional email etiquette, including clear subject lines, concise messages, and polite language.

38.7. Set Specific Times:

Allocate specific times during the day to check and respond to emails. Avoid constantly checking your inbox, which can be distracting.

38.8. Create Email Templates:

Create templates for common email responses or inquiries to save time when composing messages.

38.9. Use Keyboard Shortcuts:

Learn keyboard shortcuts for your email software to navigate and perform actions more efficiently.

38.10. Auto-Responses:

Set up auto-responses for vacations or times when you're unable to check your email promptly.

38.11. Delete Unnecessary Emails:

Regularly delete emails that are no longer needed, such as outdated messages or spam.

38.12. Flag Follow-Ups:

Flag emails that require follow-up actions, and schedule reminders to ensure you don't forget important tasks.

38.13. Archive Old Emails:

Archive emails that you want to keep but don't need in your main inbox. This helps maintain a clean inbox.

38.14. Search Efficiently:

Use search features effectively to find specific emails quickly.

38.15. Email Security:

Be cautious of phishing emails and attachments from unknown sources. Avoid clicking on suspicious links.

38.16. Encrypted Email (Optional):

Consider using encrypted email services for added security and privacy.

38.17. Email Rules:

Create email rules or filters to automatically sort and manage incoming messages.

38.18. Delegate (If Applicable):

If you're managing emails for someone else, be clear on their preferences and priorities. Delegate email responses when necessary.

38.19. Regular Cleanup:

Dedicate time to regular email cleanup and maintenance to ensure your inbox stays organized.

38.20. Continuous Learning:

Stay updated on email management best practices and new features in your email software.

Efficient email management is essential for productivity and communication in both personal and professional settings. By implementing these strategies, you can effectively manage your inbox, reduce email-related stress, and ensure that important messages are handled promptly.

39. Online Research

Online research involves gathering information, data, or insights from the internet for various purposes, including academic, professional, or personal projects. Here's a guide on how to conduct effective online research:

39.1. Define Your Research Objectives:

Clearly outline the goals and objectives of your research. What specific information are you seeking to find or answer?

39.2. Choose Reliable Sources:

Select reputable and reliable sources for your research. Academic journals, government websites, and established news outlets are often good starting points.

39.3. Use Search Engines:

Utilize popular search engines like Google, Bing, or specialized search engines for academic research like Google Scholar.

39.4. Keywords and Phrases:

Craft relevant keywords and phrases that accurately represent your research topic. Use quotation marks for exact phrases.

39.5. Advanced Search Operators:

Learn and use advanced search operators (e.g., site:, filetype:, intitle:) to refine your search results.

39.6. Evaluate Sources:

Assess the credibility of sources by considering factors like authorship, publication date, references, and the source's reputation.

39.7. Diversify Sources:

Cross-reference information from multiple sources to ensure accuracy and avoid bias.

39.8. Take Notes:

Keep detailed notes of relevant information, including source details, to cite in your research.

39.9. Organize Information:

Organize your research findings using digital tools, such as spreadsheets, note-taking apps, or reference management software.

39.10. Citation and Referencing:

Properly cite and reference sources following the appropriate citation style (e.g., APA, MLA, Chicago) for your research.

39.11. Fact-Checking:

Verify the accuracy of data and statistics by fact-checking through reputable fact-checking websites or primary sources.

39.12. Avoid Plagiarism:

Always give proper credit to the original sources by citing them correctly. Plagiarism can have serious consequences.

39.13. Stay Updated:

Keep an eye out for updates or new information related to your research topic.

39.14. Ask for Help:

If you encounter challenges or need assistance with your research, consider reaching out to librarians or subject matter experts.

39.15. Ethics and Privacy:

Respect ethical guidelines and privacy when conducting online research, especially when dealing with sensitive or personal data.

39.16. Analyze and Synthesize:

Analyze the collected data and synthesize the information to draw meaningful conclusions or insights.

39.17. Document the Process:

Keep a record of your research process, including sources explored, challenges faced, and how you resolved them.

39.18. Peer Review (Optional):

If applicable, consider having your research reviewed by peers or experts in the field for feedback and validation.

39.19. Continuous Learning:

Stay updated on research methodologies, online tools, and resources to enhance your research skills.

Effective online research is a valuable skill that can support academic pursuits, inform decision-making in professional settings, and enhance personal knowledge. By following these steps and practicing critical thinking, you can conduct thorough and reliable online research.

40. Social Media Moderation

Social media moderation involves monitoring and managing user-generated content and interactions on social media platforms to ensure a safe and respectful online environment. Whether you're moderating your own social media accounts or providing moderation services for others, here are steps to effectively manage social media content:

40.1. Define Moderation Guidelines:

Establish clear moderation guidelines or policies that outline what is acceptable and unacceptable behavior on the social media platform. This can include rules about hate speech, harassment, spam, and other violations.

40.2. Choose the Right Platforms:

Determine which social media platforms you will moderate. Different platforms may have different moderation requirements and tools.

40.3. Familiarize Yourself with Platform Tools:

Learn how to use the moderation tools provided by the social media platforms you're working with. Familiarize yourself with reporting mechanisms, blocking features, and content removal options.

40.4. Monitor Content:

Regularly monitor the content posted on the social media channels you're responsible for. Pay attention to comments, posts, messages, and mentions.

40.5. Respond to Violations:

Address violations of the moderation guidelines promptly. Remove or hide inappropriate content, warn or ban users as necessary, and provide explanations when appropriate.

40.6. Engage with Users:

Engage with users in a professional and respectful manner. Respond to questions, provide assistance, and acknowledge positive contributions.

40.7. Maintain Consistency:

Apply moderation rules consistently to ensure fairness and transparency. Avoid selective enforcement.

40.8. Escalate Serious Issues:

In cases of severe violations or threats, escalate the issue to the appropriate authoritics or platform administrators.

40.9. Protect User Privacy:

Respect and protect user privacy by not sharing personal information or engaging in any actions that may compromise it.

40.10. Stay Informed:

Stay up to date with platform policies and industry trends in social media moderation. Platforms may update their rules and tools over time.

40.11. Document Actions:

Keep a record of your moderation actions, including the date and details of each incident. This documentation can be valuable in case of disputes or audits.

40.12. Collaborate with Team Members:

If you're part of a moderation team, collaborate with colleagues to ensure a unified approach to moderation and share insights.

40.13. Community Building (Optional):

Consider fostering a sense of community by encouraging positive interactions and discussions among users.

40.14. Training (Optional):

If you're managing a team of moderators, provide training and guidance on moderation best practices and guidelines.

40.15. Review and Adapt:

Periodically review your moderation policies and strategies. Make adjustments as needed to address new challenges and user behaviors.

40.16. Crisis Management Plan (Optional):

Develop a crisis management plan to handle unexpected situations, such as social media crises or viral incidents.

40.17. Continuous Learning:

Stay informed about evolving social media trends, user behaviors, and emerging challenges in content moderation.

Effective social media moderation plays a crucial role in maintaining a positive and safe online community. By implementing these steps and staying vigilant, you can help ensure a respectful and enjoyable social media environment for users.

41. Sell Art and Photography Online

Selling art and photography online is a great way to showcase your creative work and potentially generate income. Here are steps to get started:

41.1. Create Your Art or Photography:

Produce a collection of high-quality art pieces or photographs that you want to sell. Ensure they are well-crafted and represent your unique style.

41.2. Set Up an Online Portfolio:

Create a professional website or use dedicated platforms for artists and photographers like Etsy, Fine Art America, or SmugMug. Display your work in an organized and visually appealing manner.

41.3. High-Quality Images:

Ensure that the images of your artwork or photographs are high-resolution and accurately represent the colors and details.

41.4. Write Compelling Descriptions:

Write engaging and descriptive captions or product descriptions for each piece, including details about the medium, size, and inspiration behind the work.

41.5. Pricing Strategy:

Determine your pricing strategy. Consider factors like the cost of materials, your time, and the perceived value of your art or photography.

41.6. Set Up Online Sales Channels:

Integrate e-commerce tools or platforms to facilitate online sales, including secure payment processing.

41.7. Shipping and Packaging:

Decide on your shipping and packaging methods. Ensure that your artwork or photographs are safely packaged to prevent damage during transit.

41.8. Marketing and Promotion:

Promote your work through social media, email newsletters, and collaborations with influencers or art bloggers. Build a strong online presence.

41.9. Attend Virtual Art Shows:

Explore virtual art shows and exhibitions to showcase your work to a broader audience.

41.10. SEO Optimization:

Optimize your website and product listings for search engines (SEO) to improve discoverability.

41.11. Customer Engagement:

Engage with potential buyers and existing customers through comments, emails, and social media. Build relationships with your audience.

41.12. Customer Reviews:

Encourage satisfied customers to leave reviews and testimonials on your website or platform. Positive reviews can boost your credibility.

41.13. Artistic Statement:

Craft an artistic statement or bio to share your creative journey and connect with potential buyers on a personal level.

41.14. Fulfill Orders Promptly:

Fulfill orders promptly and maintain open communication with buyers regarding shipping and delivery.

41.15. Copyright and Licensing:

Be aware of copyright and licensing considerations, especially if you plan to sell prints or digital downloads of your work.

41.16. Track Expenses and Income:

Keep detailed records of expenses related to your art or photography business. This includes materials, website hosting, marketing costs, and income from sales.

41.17. Art Shows and Galleries (Optional):

If possible, participate in local art shows, galleries, or exhibitions to gain exposure and connect with art enthusiasts.

41.18. Continuous Learning:

Stay updated on art and photography trends, techniques, and industry developments. Continuously improve your skills.

Selling art and photography online can be a fulfilling endeavor, allowing you to share your creativity with a global audience. Building a strong online presence, marketing effectively, and engaging with your audience are key to success in this competitive field.

42. Design Custom Merchandise

Creating and selling custom merchandise, such as t-shirts, mugs, and other branded products, can be a fun and profitable venture. Here's a step-by-step guide to get started:

42.1. Identify Your Niche:

Determine your target audience and niche for your custom merchandise. Who are you designing for, and what types of products will they be interested in?

42.2. Research Market Trends:

Research current market trends and identify popular designs and themes within your chosen niche.

42.3. Create Unique Designs:

Develop eye-catching and original designs that resonate with your target audience. You can use graphic design software or hire a designer if needed.

42.4. Choose Merchandise Types:

Decide on the types of merchandise you want to offer, such as t-shirts, hoodies, stickers, or accessories. Consider the quality and variety of products.

42.5. Print-on-Demand Services:

Explore print-on-demand services like Printful, Printify, or Teespring that allow you to create custom products without holding inventory.

42.6. Create an Online Store:

Set up an e-commerce website or use platforms like Shopify, WooCommerce, or Etsy to create an online store for your merchandise.

42.7. Product Listings:

Create appealing product listings with high-quality images, detailed descriptions, and pricing information.

42.8. Branding and Packaging:

Develop a strong brand identity, including a logo and branding elements. Consider custom packaging for a professional touch.

42.9. Pricing Strategy:

Determine your pricing strategy by factoring in production costs, profit margins, and market competition.

42.10. Payment and Shipping:

Set up secure payment processing options and define your shipping policies. Calculate shipping costs accurately.

42.11. Legal Considerations:

Be aware of copyright and trademark issues when designing merchandise. Ensure your designs do not infringe on others' intellectual property.

42.12. Marketing Plan:

Create a comprehensive marketing plan to promote your merchandise. Use social media, email marketing, and influencer collaborations to reach your audience.

42.13. Website Optimization:

Optimize your website for search engines (SEO) to increase visibility in search results.

42.14. Analytics and Feedback:

Use analytics tools to track website traffic, sales, and customer behavior. Collect and analyze feedback from customers.

42.15. Customer Support:

Provide excellent customer support by addressing inquiries, handling returns, and resolving issues promptly.

42.16. Expand Your Product Line:

Consider expanding your product offerings as your brand grows. Introduce new designs and merchandise.

42.17. Collaborate and Network:

Collaborate with other creators or businesses to cross-promote and expand your reach.

42.18. Inventory Management (If Applicable):

If you choose to hold inventory, manage your stock efficiently to avoid overstock or shortages.

42.19. Continuous Learning:

Stay updated on design trends, e-commerce strategies, and customer preferences to adapt and grow your business.

Selling custom merchandise requires creativity, marketing skills, and a deep understanding of your target audience. With the right approach and dedication, you can build a successful custom merchandise business and turn your creative designs into a thriving venture.

43. Voice Acting and Audio Narration

Voice acting and audio narration involve using your voice to bring characters, stories, and scripts to life through audio recordings. Whether you're pursuing this as a hobby or a career, here are the steps to get started:

43.1. Develop Your Voice:

Practice and refine your vocal skills. Work on your pronunciation, tone, pitch, and enunciation. Consider taking voice lessons if needed.

43.2. Choose a Niche:

Identify the type of voice acting or narration you want to specialize in. Options include audiobook narration, animation voiceovers, commercial voiceovers, and more.

43.3. Create a Recording Space:

Set up a quiet and acoustically treated space for recording. Invest in a quality microphone, headphones, and audio recording software.

43.4. Build a Portfolio:

Create a portfolio or demo reel showcasing your voice talent. Include samples that demonstrate your versatility and skills in various genres.

43.5. Develop Character Voices:

If you're interested in character work, practice creating distinct voices for different characters. This can be essential for animation or video game voice acting.

43.6. Training and Education:

Consider taking voice acting workshops or courses to enhance your skills and learn from professionals in the industry.

43.7. Audition for Roles:

Look for voice acting auditions on websites like Voices.com, Voice123, or Casting Call Club. Audition for projects that match your skills and interests.

43.8. Home Recording:

Record audition samples and projects from your home studio. Ensure high-quality recordings free from background noise.

43.9. Networking:

Connect with other voice actors, producers, and directors in the industry. Networking can lead to opportunities and collaborations.

43.10. Online Presence:

Create a professional online presence through a personal website or profiles on platforms like LinkedIn, SoundCloud, and social media.

43.11. Market Yourself:

Promote your voice acting services through online marketing, email outreach, and showcasing your work on platforms like YouTube or Vimeo.

43.12. Copyright and Licensing:

Be aware of copyright and licensing issues when working with scripts, characters, or copyrighted material.

43.13. Pricing and Contracts:

Determine your pricing structure for voice acting services. Draft clear contracts with clients to outline terms, payment, and usage rights.

43.14. Continuous Practice:

Keep honing your craft by practicing regularly, experimenting with different accents and styles, and seeking feedback.

43.15. Build a Reputation:

Deliver high-quality work on time and build a reputation for professionalism and reliability.

43.16. Voice Acting Communities:

Join online voice acting communities and forums to stay informed about industry trends and opportunities.

43.17. Voiceover Agents (Optional):

Consider working with a voiceover agent who can help you find auditions and negotiate contracts on your behalf.

43.18. Audition Etiquette:

Learn audition etiquette, which includes following instructions carefully and delivering auditions promptly.

Voice acting and audio narration can be a rewarding career or creative outlet for those with a passion for storytelling and a unique vocal talent. Success in this field often comes from continuous practice, networking, and a commitment to delivering compelling performances.

44. Virtual Event DJ

Becoming a virtual event DJ allows you to entertain audiences through live-streamed events, parties, conferences, and more. Here's how to start your journey as a virtual event DJ:

44.1. Develop DJ Skills:

If you're not already an experienced DJ, learn the fundamentals of DJing, including beatmatching, mixing, and using DJ software and equipment.

44.2. Choose Your Equipment:

Invest in quality DJ equipment, including a mixer, turntables or controllers, headphones, and a computer with DJ software.

44.3. Build a Music Library:

Create a diverse music library spanning different genres and styles to cater to various event preferences.

44.4. Learn Virtual DJ Software:

Familiarize yourself with virtual DJ software that allows you to live-stream your performances, such as OBS Studio or Streamlabs OBS.

44.5. Set Up Your Virtual Studio:

Design and set up a visually appealing virtual studio or DJ booth where you'll be broadcasting your live streams.

44.6. Acquire Streaming Hardware:

Invest in streaming hardware, including a webcam, microphone, and audio interface, to ensure high-quality audio and video during your streams.

44.7. Select Streaming Platforms:

Choose the platforms where you'll broadcast your virtual DJ sets. Popular options include Twitch, YouTube Live, Facebook Live, and Mixcloud Live.

44.8. Promote Your Brand:

Create a strong online presence through social media, a website, and promotional materials that showcase your brand as a virtual event DJ.

44.9. Set Pricing and Packages:

Determine your pricing structure for virtual DJ services, whether it's hourly rates or packages for specific types of events.

44.10. Legal Considerations:

Ensure you have the necessary licenses to play copyrighted music during your live streams to avoid copyright infringement.

44.11. Network and Collaborate:

Build connections in the virtual event industry and collaborate with event planners, organizers, and other professionals.

44.12. Plan Your Sets:

Prepare and plan your DJ sets for specific events, considering the audience and theme of the event.

44.13. Engage with Your Audience:

Interact with viewers during your live streams by responding to comments, requests, and shout-outs.

44.14. Test and Rehearse:

Before going live, conduct test runs to ensure all your equipment and software are working correctly.

44.15. Marketing and Promotion:

Promote your upcoming virtual DJ events through social media, email newsletters, and your website.

44.16. Technical Support:

Be prepared to troubleshoot technical issues that may arise during live streams.

44.17. Collect Feedback:

Gather feedback from your audience and clients to improve your virtual DJ services.

44.18. Continuous Learning:

Stay updated on DJing trends, technology, and streaming platforms to enhance your skills.

Becoming a virtual event DJ requires a combination of DJing skills, technical knowledge, and online marketing. As virtual events continue to gain popularity, there's ample opportunity to entertain and engage with audiences worldwide from the comfort of your own virtual DJ booth.

45. Online Karaoke Hosting

Online karaoke hosting allows you to bring the joy of karaoke to virtual audiences by organizing and hosting karaoke sessions over the internet. Here's a step-by-step guide to becoming an online karaoke host:

45.1. Equip Yourself:

Ensure you have the necessary equipment, including a computer, a microphone, headphones, and a stable internet connection.

45.2. Choose a Platform:

Select a platform for hosting your online karaoke sessions. Popular options include Zoom, Twitch, YouTube Live, or specialized karaoke platforms like Karafun or Smule.

45.3. Licensing and Copyright:

Be aware of copyright laws and licensing requirements for hosting karaoke sessions. Obtain necessary licenses if you plan to use copyrighted songs.

45.4. Set a Schedule:

Determine a regular schedule for your online karaoke sessions. Consistency can help build an audience.

45.5. Build a Song Library:

Compile a diverse song library that includes a wide range of genres and songs to cater to different tastes.

45.6. Promote Your Sessions:

Use social media, online communities, and your website to promote your online karaoke sessions. Create event pages and share links to your streams.

45.7. Set Up a Virtual Stage:

Design and decorate a virtual stage or backdrop for your karaoke sessions to create a fun and engaging atmosphere.

45.8. Technical Setup:

Familiarize yourself with the technical aspects of your chosen platform, including streaming settings, screen sharing, and audio configuration.

45.9. Practice and Rehearse:

Rehearse your hosting skills, including interacting with participants, managing requests, and troubleshooting technical issues.

45.10. Hosting Etiquette:

Learn how to be an engaging and supportive host, encouraging participants, and creating a positive atmosphere.

45.11. Interactive Features:

Explore interactive features like chat, polls, and contests to engage with your audience during karaoke sessions.

45.12. Song Requests:

Establish a system for song requests, whether it's through chat, email, or a dedicated request platform.

45.13. Song Lyrics and Displays:

Display song lyrics on-screen using screen sharing or dedicated karaoke software so participants can sing along.

45.14. Copyright Compliance:

Ensure you comply with copyright laws when streaming or displaying lyrics for copyrighted songs.

45.15. Engage with Participants:

Interact with your audience by acknowledging song dedications, celebrating participants' performances, and fostering a sense of community.

45.16. Moderation:

Set guidelines and moderate your online karaoke sessions to ensure a respectful and enjoyable experience for all participants.

45.17. Monetization (Optional):

Consider monetizing your online karaoke sessions through donations, subscriptions, or paid requests.

45.18. Continuous Improvement:

Collect feedback from participants and use it to improve your hosting skills and the overall quality of your karaoke sessions.

45.19. Legal Consultation (Optional):

If your online karaoke hosting business grows significantly, consult with legal experts to ensure compliance with copyright and licensing regulations.

Online karaoke hosting is an entertaining and interactive way to connect with people worldwide and share the joy of singing. With the right preparation, technical knowledge, and hosting skills, you can create memorable and enjoyable karaoke experiences for your virtual audience.

46. Microtasking and Gig Economy Platforms

Microtasking and gig economy platforms provide opportunities for individuals to earn money by completing short, often one-time tasks or gigs. Here's how to get started in this flexible and diverse field:

46.1. Research Platforms:

Explore popular microtasking and gig economy platforms like Amazon Mechanical Turk, Upwork, Fiverr, TaskRabbit, Gigwalk, and more. Understand the types of tasks each platform offers.

46.2. Identify Your Skills:

Assess your skills and talents to determine what type of tasks or services you can offer. This can include writing, graphic design, data entry, coding, virtual assistance, and more.

46.3. Create a Profile:

Register on your chosen platform(s) and create a compelling profile. Highlight your skills, experience, and qualifications.

46.4. Verify Payment Methods:

Ensure that you have a verified and secure payment method set up on the platform to receive payments for completed tasks.

46.5. Browse Tasks/Gigs:

Browse available tasks or gigs on the platform. Filter by your skills and interests to find opportunities that match your capabilities.

46.6. Apply or Bid:

Submit proposals or bids for tasks or gigs that interest you. Tailor your pitches to showcase your suitability for the job.

46.7. Pricing Strategy:

Determine your pricing strategy based on factors such as your skill level, market rates, and the complexity of the task.

46.8. Deliver High-Quality Work:

Once you secure a task or gig, ensure that you deliver high-quality work within the agreed-upon timeframe.

46.9. Communicate Effectively:

Maintain clear and prompt communication with clients or task posters. Address any questions or concerns promptly.

46.10. Build a Portfolio:

As you complete tasks or gigs, build a portfolio showcasing your work. This can help attract more clients in the future.

46.11. Reviews and Ratings:

Encourage clients to leave reviews and ratings for your work. Positive feedback can boost your credibility.

46.12. Time Management:

Manage your time effectively to juggle multiple tasks or gigs if you're working on a freelance basis.

46.13. Upskill:

Continuously improve your skills and stay updated with industry trends to remain competitive in the gig economy.

46.14. Manage Finances:

Keep track of your earnings, expenses, and taxes. Consider consulting with a financial advisor or accountant if needed.

46.15. Protect Yourself:

Be cautious of potential scams or fraudulent clients. Verify the legitimacy of offers and use secure payment methods.

46.16. Networking:

Connect with other freelancers or gig workers in your field. Networking can lead to collaborations and referrals.

46.17. Diversify Income Streams:

Explore opportunities on multiple platforms to diversify your income streams and reduce dependency on a single platform.

46.18. Set Goals:

Set financial and career goals to motivate yourself and track your progress in the gig economy.

46.19. Legal Considerations:

Be aware of legal and contractual obligations when working with clients. Read and understand platform terms and conditions.

46.20. Continuous Learning:

Stay adaptable and open to learning new skills and adapting to evolving gig economy trends.

The gig economy offers a wide range of opportunities for individuals with various skills and interests. By strategically choosing platforms, delivering quality work, and effectively managing your freelance career, you can find success and financial stability in this dynamic field.

47. Cashback and Rewards Programs

Cashback and rewards programs allow you to earn money or receive various benefits while making everyday purchases. Here's a guide on how to make the most of these programs:

47.1. Research Programs:

Explore different cashback and rewards programs available in your region. These can include credit card rewards, cashback apps, loyalty programs, and more.

47.2. Credit Card Rewards:

If you have a credit card, review its rewards program. Some credit cards offer cashback, points, or miles for every dollar spent.

47.3. Sign Up:

Register for the cashback or rewards programs that align with your spending habits and financial goals.

47.4. Understand Terms and Conditions:

Familiarize yourself with the terms and conditions of each program. Pay attention to earning rates, redemption options, and any fees associated with participation.

47.5. Link Payment Methods:

Connect your credit cards, debit cards, or payment methods to the relevant rewards apps or platforms.

47.6. Shop Smart:

When shopping online or in-store, use your linked payment methods to earn cashback or rewards automatically.

47.7. Stack Rewards:

Maximize your earnings by stacking rewards. For example, use a cashback credit card for purchases, and also use a cashback app or browser extension for additional savings.

47.8. Track Spending:

Monitor your spending to ensure it aligns with your budget. Avoid overspending just to earn rewards.

47.9. Redemption Options:

Explore the various ways to redeem your rewards. Options may include cashback, gift cards, travel discounts, merchandise, or charitable donations.

47.10. Redeem Strategically:

Plan your redemptions strategically to get the most value from your rewards. For example, use travel rewards for a vacation or cashback to offset bills.

47.11. Refer Friends:

Many rewards programs offer referral bonuses. Invite friends and family to join to earn additional rewards.

47.12. Pay Bills:

Some rewards programs allow you to earn rewards by paying bills or utilities through their platforms.

47.13. Stay Informed:

Keep an eye on special promotions or bonus offers that can boost your rewards earnings.

47.14. Mobile Wallets:

Use mobile wallets like Apple Pay or Google Pay to earn rewards and simplify payments.

47.15. Protect Your Data:

Be cautious about sharing personal information with rewards programs. Review their privacy policies and opt-out of data sharing if necessary.

47.16. Credit Score Management:

Be responsible with credit card use. Pay your balances in full and on time to maintain a good credit score.

47.17. Automate Savings:

Consider automating a portion of your cashback or rewards earnings into a savings or investment account.

47.18. Avoid Debt:

While cashback and rewards are beneficial, avoid overspending or carrying credit card balances that can lead to debt.

47.19. Review and Update:

Periodically review your rewards programs to ensure they still align with your financial goals and spending patterns. Update as needed.

Cashback and rewards programs can be a valuable way to save money and enjoy additional benefits from your everyday spending. By understanding the programs, using them strategically, and being mindful of your financial habits, you can make the most of these opportunities.

48. Online Contests and Competitions

Participating in online contests and competitions can be a fun way to showcase your skills, talents, or creativity and potentially win prizes. Here's a guide to get started:

48.1. Identify Your Interests and Skills:

Determine what you're passionate about and where your skills or talents lie. This will help you choose the right contests to enter.

48.2. Research Contests:

Look for online contests and competitions related to your interests. These can include art contests, writing competitions, photography contests, coding challenges, and more.

48.3. Read Rules and Guidelines:

Carefully read the rules, guidelines, and eligibility criteria for each contest you're interested in. Ensure you meet all requirements.

48.4. Create or Prepare Your Entry:

Depending on the contest, prepare your entry. This might involve creating artwork, writing a story, developing software, or any other relevant task.

48.5. Review Past Winners:

Study previous winners or successful entries to understand the quality and style expected by the judges or organizers.

48.6. Submission Process:

Follow the submission process outlined in the contest rules. Pay attention to deadlines and any required documents or forms.

48.7. Promote Your Entry:

If the contest allows or encourages public voting, promote your entry through social media, email, and your network to garner votes or support.

48.8. Engage with the Community:

Participate in the contest's online community, forums, or social media groups to connect with fellow contestants and gain insights.

48.9. Protect Your Work:

If your entry involves original content, consider copyright and licensing implications. Watermark your images or add copyright notices if necessary.

48.10. Submit Multiple Entries (If Allowed):

If the contest allows multiple entries, submit more than one to increase your chances of winning.

48.11. Stay Informed:

Keep an eye on updates and announcements from the contest organizers. They may provide valuable information or extend deadlines.

48.12. Collaborate (If Applicable):

Some contests allow or require team entries. Collaborate with others who share your interests and skills.

48.13. Be Gracious in Defeat:

Remember that competition is tough, and not everyone can win. If you don't win, take it as an opportunity to learn and improve.

48.14. Collect Feedback:

Seek feedback on your entry from friends, mentors, or experts to refine your skills for future contests.

48.15. Review Your Results:

If you win or receive recognition, review the judges' feedback or comments to understand what impressed them.

48.16. Network and Build Connections:

Use the experience to connect with others in your field and build a network of like-minded individuals.

48.17. Stay Persistent:

Don't be discouraged by losses. Continue participating in contests to hone your skills and increase your chances of success.

48.18. Share Your Achievements:

Publicize your wins and achievements on your online portfolio, resume, or social media profiles to showcase your skills and credibility.

Online contests and competitions can offer recognition, prizes, and a sense of accomplishment. By selecting contests aligned with your interests, following the rules, and continuously improving your skills, you can increase your chances of success in the online competition arena.

49. Pet Sitting and Dog Walking Apps

Pet sitting and dog walking apps provide opportunities to earn money by taking care of pets while their owners are away or busy. Here's a guide on how to get started with these apps:

49.1. Research and Choose Apps:

Research pet sitting and dog walking apps available in your area. Popular ones include Rover, Wag!, PetSitter.com, and Care.com.

49.2. Create a Profile:

Sign up on the chosen app and create a detailed profile. Include information about your experience with pets, services you offer, availability, and rates.

49.3. Verify Your Identity:

Many apps require identity verification and background checks to ensure the safety of pets and owners. Complete these verification steps.

49.4. Set Your Rates:

Determine your pricing for services such as dog walking, pet sitting, or house sitting. Consider local rates and your level of experience.

49.5. Write an Engaging Bio:

Write a compelling bio that showcases your love for animals and your commitment to their well-being.

49.6. Upload High-Quality Photos:

Include high-quality photos of yourself, any pets you own, and images of your home if you plan to offer pet sitting services in your own space.

49.7. Availability and Schedule:

Specify your availability, including the days and times you can offer your services. Be clear about your schedule to manage client expectations.

49.8. Services Offered:

Clearly outline the services you offer, such as dog walking, pet feeding, grooming, or overnight stays.

49.9. Communication:

Maintain open and timely communication with potential clients. Respond to messages promptly.

49.10. Meet and Greet:

Arrange meet-and-greet sessions with pet owners and their pets before accepting bookings. This helps establish trust and ensures a good fit.

49.11. Safety and Care:

Prioritize the safety and well-being of the pets in your care. Follow the owner's instructions regarding feeding, medication, exercise, and any specific needs.

49.12. Insurance and Liability:

Review the app's policies on insurance and liability coverage. Some apps offer insurance to protect you and the pets you care for.

49.13. Secure Payment:

Use the app's payment system to ensure secure and timely payment for your services.

49.14. Client Reviews:

Encourage satisfied clients to leave reviews and ratings on the app. Positive reviews can boost your credibility.

49.15. Marketing (Optional):

Promote your services on social media, through word-of-mouth referrals, or by creating business cards to share with local pet owners.

49.16. Pet First Aid Knowledge:

Consider taking a pet first aid and CPR course to be prepared for emergencies.

49.17. Be Professional:

Maintain professionalism in all your interactions with clients. Respect their homes and their pets.

49.18. Continuous Learning:

Stay informed about pet care trends and best practices, especially if you plan to offer specialized services.

49.19. Build a Client Base:

Over time, build a roster of loyal clients who trust you with their pets.

49.20. Legal Considerations:

Familiarize yourself with any local regulations or licensing requirements for pet sitting and dog walking services.

Pet sitting and dog walking can be a rewarding way to spend time with animals and earn income. By creating a comprehensive profile, providing excellent care, and ensuring safety and communication, you can build a successful pet care business through these apps.

Testing websites and apps for usability involves evaluating their user-friendliness and identifying areas for improvement. Here's a guide on how to start a career in usability testing:

50. Testing Websites and Apps for Usability

50.1. Develop Basic Skills:

Gain a fundamental understanding of usability principles and user experience (UX) design. Familiarize yourself with common usability testing methods.

50.2. Build a Testing Toolkit:

Acquire the necessary tools and software for usability testing, such as screen recording software, eye-tracking devices, and usability testing platforms.

50.3. Study UX Design:

Consider taking online courses or certifications in UX design to deepen your knowledge and skills in user-centered design principles.

50.4. Create a Portfolio:

Begin building a portfolio of usability testing projects. Document your process, findings, and recommendations for each project.

50.5. Sign Up for Testing Platforms:

Register on usability testing platforms like UserTesting, UserZoom, or TryMyUI, which connect testers with companies looking for usability feedback.

50.6. Set Up a Professional Profile:

Create a professional profile on usability testing platforms, highlighting your skills and expertise.

50.7. Participate in Tests:

Start participating in usability tests offered through the platforms. Follow instructions carefully and provide detailed feedback.

50.8. Record Your Sessions:

Use screen recording software to capture your testing sessions. This will help you provide evidence and reference points in your feedback.

50.9. Offer Constructive Feedback:

Provide constructive and actionable feedback to the companies you work with. Focus on usability issues and suggestions for improvement.

50.10. Communication Skills:

Develop strong communication skills to effectively convey your findings and recommendations.

50.11. Time Management:

Manage your time efficiently to complete tests within the specified timeframe.

50.12. Maintain Professionalism:

Be professional and respectful in all your interactions with clients and testing platforms.

50.13. Build Your Reputation:

Accumulate positive reviews and ratings on usability testing platforms to increase your visibility and chances of getting more opportunities.

50.14. Seek Feedback:

Request feedback from clients on your usability testing reports to continuously improve your skills.

50.15. Continuous Learning:

Stay updated on the latest trends in usability testing and UX design through books, blogs, webinars, and conferences.

50.16. Expand Your Services (Optional):

Consider offering additional services like usability audits, user interviews, or heuristic evaluations to broaden your expertise.

50.17. Networking:

Connect with UX designers, researchers, and professionals in the field to learn from their experiences and gain insights.

50.18. Market Your Services (Freelancers):

If you choose to work as a freelance usability tester, market your services through personal websites, social media, and networking.

50.19. Legal Considerations:

Understand the legal and ethical responsibilities of usability testing, including user consent, data privacy, and confidentiality.

50.20. Join UX Communities:

Participate in UX and usability testing communities to share knowledge, ask questions, and stay engaged in the field.

Usability testing is essential for creating user-friendly websites and apps. By honing your skills, building a strong portfolio, and networking in the UX community, you can establish a successful career in usability testing and contribute to improving digital experiences for users.

Conclusion

In conclusion, this book has explored 50 diverse ways to earn money online, ranging from online marketplaces and freelance work to creative pursuits and digital services. We've touched on opportunities for individuals with varying levels of expertise, from those seeking quick side income to those aspiring to build full-fledged online careers.

The digital landscape is vast and ever-evolving, providing a wealth of options for those looking to harness the power of the internet for financial gain. Whether you're interested in selling products, offering services, or sharing your creativity and knowledge, there's a path for you in the online world.

It's important to remember that success in any online endeavour often requires dedication, continuous learning, and adaptability. Additionally, ethical and legal considerations, such as copyright and privacy, should always be upheld.

As you embark on your journey to earn money online, keep in mind that it's not just about the financial rewards. It's an opportunity to express your passion, develop new skills, connect with a global audience, and, ultimately, achieve your personal and financial goals.

No matter which avenue you choose, the possibilities in the online realm are vast and waiting for you to explore. So, take the knowledge and inspiration you've gained from this eBook, set your goals, and dive into the world of online opportunities. The digital landscape is yours to conquer.